ANXIOUSLY ATTACHED

ANXIOUSLY ATTACHED
Understanding and Working with Preoccupied Attachment

Edited by
Linda Cundy

R Routledge
Taylor & Francis Group

LONDON AND NEW YORK

First published 2017 by
Karnac Books Ltd.

Published 2018 by Routledge
2 Park Square, Milton Park, Abingdon, Oxon OX14 4RN
711 Third Avenue, New York, NY 10017, USA

Routledge is an imprint of the Taylor & Francis Group, an informa business

British Library Cataloguing in Publication Data

A C.I.P. for this book is available from the British Library

ISBN-13: 9781782205197 (pbk)

Typeset by Medlar Publishing Solutions Pvt Ltd, India

CONTENTS

ACKNOWLEDGEMENTS

This monograph comprises four papers originally presented at a one-day conference at the Wimbledon Guild in February 2016.

John Priestley, the Head of Talking Therapies at Wimbledon Guild, had anticipated the value of attachment theory as an empirical body of knowledge on which to base clinical work at a time when it was still considered of rather fringe importance. Sixteen years later, this conference was the product of his pioneering vision of the role Wimbledon Guild might play in furthering attachment theory—he proposed the theme having noticed the difficulties we so often encounter in therapeutic work with clients who are "anxiously attached". I am deeply grateful to him for his vision of the Wimbledon Guild as a centre for promoting the work of John Bowlby and others who have developed those initial concerns with relational bonds, maternal deprivation, separation, and loss. The Wimbledon Guild continues to champion attachment theory, offering one-day seminars, eight-day courses, and now two diplomas, one in attachment-based counselling (unique in the UK) and a postgraduate diploma in attachment-based therapy.

The conference was organised by Amanda Glass with her usual efficiency and flair. That it caught the attention of so many delegates can be credited to Amanda's skills at promoting events, and that the auditorium was transformed on the day with banners and flowers into an attractive environment is testament to her eye for detail.

I also wish to thank Wendy Pridmore, Chief Executive at Wimbledon Guild, and Georgina Hoare, the current Head of Talking Therapies, for their continuing support for the attachment programme. Thanks too to the technicians who supported speakers on the day and the volunteers whose assistance contributed to a successful event.

Of course, my particular appreciation goes to the speakers themselves, who each contributed original work to help us all reflect on anxious attachment: how it develops and is experienced between mothers and babies, in adult couple relationships, and in the consulting room. They have been generous with their time, not only in preparing and presenting such stimulating material on the day, but then in undertaking the extra work needed to transform their presentations into papers for this monograph—I am most grateful for their willingness to engage in the process of writing and editing.

Finally, I am deeply grateful to Maggie Turp, who chaired the conference with her customary skill and thoughtfulness, facilitating discussion in a spirit of respect for different perspectives. Maggie has also kindly contributed the introduction to this collection.

I hope you enjoy reading these contributions on anxious/preoccupied attachment and that you find them useful in helping to think about clinically challenging situations, and I hope to see you at a future Wimbledon Guild attachment conference.

Linda Cundy (editor)

ABOUT THE EDITOR AND CONTRIBUTORS

Linda Cundy is an attachment-based psychoanalytic psychotherapist and supervisor with a private practice. She has run courses on attachment at the Wimbledon Guild for sixteen years, and these are now offered as a Post-Graduate Diploma in Attachment-Based Therapy, of which Linda is lead tutor. She has taught at several psychotherapy organisations. A book, *Love in the Age of the Internet: Attachment in the Digital Era* (Karnac, 2015), was written/edited by Linda.

Steve Farnfield is a senior lecturer and convenor of the MSc in Attachment Studies at the University of Roehampton. He is a social worker and play therapist, and licensed trainer for various Dynamic Maturational Model attachment assessment procedures, including the Adult Attachment Interview. Steve is author of the Child Attachment and Play Assessment, a new method of analysing children's story stems for attachment strategy and unresolved trauma. His interests include child and adult attachment in the context of family stress, child maltreatment, fostering, and adoption. With Paul Holmes, he is co-editor of the three-volume *Routledge Handbooks of Attachment*.

Amanda Jones is a consultant perinatal psychotherapist and professional lead of North East London NHS Foundation Trust's Perinatal Parent–Infant Mental Health Service. She trained as a family therapist and pursued her doctoral research at the Tavistock Centre/University of East London. In collaboration with the Anna Freud Centre, Amanda was the therapist in the Channel Four documentaries *Help Me Love My Baby*, and she has recently made five further documentaries with the NSPCC and Warwick Medical School. She contributes in several governmental policy groups to try to enhance understanding about the importance of early intervention.

Anne Power trained in attachment-based psychoanalytic psychotherapy at the Bowlby Centre and did an MA in supervision at WPF/Roehampton. She trained in couple work with Relate. She has taught in a number of settings since 2000, and is currently a supervisor and visiting lecturer at Regents University London. Previously, her work was in the NHS and voluntary agencies; she now has a private practice in central London for couples and individuals. She is UKCP and BACP registered.

Maggie Turp is a practitioner psychologist and analytically trained psychotherapist and supervisor. She is a visiting lecturer at the Tavistock and Portman NHS Trust and an independent trainer offering workshops on the effects of trauma on self-narrative, the physical expression of psychological distress, and the psychology of climate change. She has published several journal papers and two books, *Psychosomatic Health: The Body and the Word* (Palgrave, 2001) and *Hidden Self-Harm: Narratives from Psychotherapy* (Jessica Kingsley, 2003).

INTRODUCTION

Maggie Turp

This book, like the conference out of which it emerged, revolves around the particular way of being in the world and relating to others characteristic of preoccupied attachment. In the first chapter, Linda Cundy sets the scene with an outline of the phenomenon under discussion, via her evocation of an archetypal preoccupied patient, Archie. Archie's internal world is "filled with anxious fretting and grievance". He is resentful, easily offended, and constantly on the lookout for signs of rejection. His needs are apparently insatiable. A particular conundrum for the psychotherapist resides in Archie's difficulty in making use of the therapeutic relationship. As Cundy notes, "Rather than internalising the care and attention he receives, he remains focused on what is missing". Archie's difficulties are understood as having their origins in disturbed early attachment relationships of a particular kind. Recognition of the reality and nature of such disturbances form the common ground shared by and investigated by all four contributors to this volume.

There are, of course, many different ways of thinking about and coming to understand a phenomenon. Psychoanalytic modes of understanding have evolved primarily on the basis of conversation, correspondence, and reflection on themes that have emerged in clinical work. Attachment theory, in keeping with its roots in the natural sciences, has proceeded by way of observational and ethological studies to standardised protocols such as the Strange Situation Test and qualitative research using the Adult Attachment Interview. These differences notwithstanding, there are—and always have been—significant areas of overlap. Clinical concerns have always been a part of the attachment field of interest, and John Bowlby, the founder of attachment theory, had a background in psychoanalysis and child analysis. Freud drew on scientific research, art, and philosophy in his work as well as on clinical material, and the psychoanalytic method has expanded to include other roads to understanding, for example close, home-based observation of infant development and, more recently, qualitative and quantitative studies of clinical outcomes. Historically, however, the different emphases and paths of development have militated against each approach enjoying the full benefit of the emerging understandings and insights of the other.

This situation has changed substantially as time has gone on. Among the many practitioners and researchers who have contributed to the softening of the boundaries and promulgation of mutual understanding, Peter Fonagy merits special mention in relation to the bridging role of the theory of mentalization. The development of neuroscience, and the emergence of findings that underpin the validity of key attachment and psychoanalytic claims, has also helped to bridge two related yet different means of understanding. For example, in relation to attachment, neuroscience has provided hard evidence of the truth of the attachment narrative in terms of its implications for brain development. In relation to the psychoanalytic emphasis on the power of the unconscious, neuroscience has established beyond doubt that most mental processing takes place beneath the level of consciousness.

Another landmark has been reached with the conference that gave rise to this book, where an object relations psychotherapist, two attachment-based psychotherapists, and an attachment researcher were able to come together to share a platform and each, in his or her own way, address the theme of preoccupied attachment. As a consequence, and for the first time, it has been possible to produce a book revolving around a scenario recognisable to practitioners everywhere that brings together a clinical account by object relations parent–infant therapist, Amanda Jones; reflections by two attachment-based practitioners, Linda Cundy and Anne Power; and findings in the form of charts and diagrams, as well as extracts from Child and Adult Attachment Interviews, by attachment researcher Steve Farnfield, whose work is informed by the Dynamic Maturational Model (Crittenden, 2000). This theoretical pluralism brings with it a range of perspectives, each of which throws a particular light on the preoccupied mode of relating, and each chapter contributes in its own way to our evolving understanding.

* * *

The importance of furthering and deepening our understanding is underlined by Linda Cundy as she draws our attention to the frequency with which "preoccupied" patients present for psychotherapy and the unfortunate tendency for the therapy to "get stuck or end badly". Having introduced us to Archie, a fictional character based on features of many anxiously attached clients, she delineates a range of predisposing scenarios with the potential to push an individual towards a preoccupied style of relating. She highlights in particular the core anxiety of being abandoned and the recognisable, albeit problematic, patterns of defence aimed at preventing the feared abandonment. Among these is the pushing of boundaries by the patient in an attempt, whether conscious or unconscious, to "be special" and "to be made an exception". Cundy describes patients who arrive early, leave late, seek out contact between sessions, ask personal questions, bring gifts, and—in the case of one patient—linger in her bathroom, opening and closing cupboard doors and presumably making a close inspection of the toiletries and medicines inside.

Incidents such as these raise the question of when special therapeutic accommodations or departures from "normal" techniques are necessary for the building of a therapeutic alliance, and when they constitute, as Cundy writes, "a re-enactment of an unpredictable relationship with chaotic boundaries". Many of us will recognise the dilemma. On the one hand, normal holding of boundaries may be experienced as hostility and abandonment, with the result that the patient does not continue the therapy. On the other, adapting the boundaries may be experienced as a kind of collusion. Without claiming to offer a solution, Cundy demonstrates her capacity to keep thinking under the extreme pressures that these patients bring to bear, a capacity sustained by a theoretical approach that enables her to conceptualise the unconscious processes that affect preoccupied patients and, by extension, those in personal and professional contact with them.

The second half of Cundy's chapter comprises a clear and detailed outline of what she sees as the specific aims of therapy with preoccupied clients. The ten points she sets out arguably constitute a useful checklist for the aims of therapy with *all* clients. However, in her elaboration of each theme, she clarifies the particular way in which an aim, for example assistance with mourning, plays out in the case of a preoccupied client. There is much food for thought here, and a useful guide for the therapist struggling for clarity in the face of the complex countertransference experience stirred up by the preoccupied patient.

* * *

The focus in Amanda Jones' chapter is not on the adult individual but on the perinatal period, the "precious and precarious time span" that stretches from the moment of conception to toddlerhood: "The perinatal period is precious because it offers hope, new life, and potential for growth for everyone involved, but it is also precarious because it is a time of enhanced vulnerability both physically and emotionally." Jones' chapter explores the way in which the arrival of the baby activates the new mother's "painful pre-existing vulnerabilities, hurts, and resentments". These are given new life, and the associated defensive structure may be dangerous, even life-threatening, for the baby.

Parent–infant psychotherapy is a relatively new development in the field of object relations. Historically, it is in the field of attachment studies that a greater emphasis has been placed on wider social questions. An early example that springs to mind is the work of James and Joyce Robertson, who were colleagues of John Bowlby and whose films transformed the situation with regard to parents visiting their sick children in hospital. Parent–infant therapy also addresses a wider social question: how can we intervene in a preventive, protective way, so that the distress and deprivation of one generation is not unconsciously transmitted to the next, with all the negative individual and social consequences that follow? This concern with anticipating and intervening to prevent potential disturbance is very much in keeping with Bowlby's mission.

Having explored the terrain, Jones offers a detailed description of her work with a mother, Sarah, and her baby, Maisie. In a moving and sometimes harrowing account, Jones brings the reader into close contact with the very difficult feelings that arise in the countertransference during the course of the work. While other approaches to working with mothers who have difficulty in parenting tend to avoid consideration of the powerful feelings stirred up in those who try to help, Jones writes in the psychoanalytic tradition of attending and giving voice to such feelings. For Jones, this is not only a matter of guarding against enactments but also an opportunity for the patient to benefit from the experience of being with a therapist who can continue to think in the face of terror, rage, and despair. "While absorbing emotional material, the therapist will be affected. The task is to try to understand what is occurring. For both parent and baby, hopefully, confusing and unbearable emotional states will be experienced as, somehow, cared for and survived."

* * *

In her chapter, Jones questions the value of attachment categories, citing Fonagy's reference to attachment researchers who "appear to reify attachment categories, considering them as theoretical entities rather than observed clusters of behavior". Her preference is for a psychoanalytic perspective that, as Fonagy puts it, "might encourage us to think less categorically and more dimensionally about attachment security" (Fonagy, 2001, p. 187). By contrast, Steve Farnfield's area of interest and expertise is the close investigation of the fine detail and textural qualities of attachment categories. A creative tension emerges between the helpfulness of a defined category and a detailed profile, on the one hand, and the risk of losing sight of the unique quality of an individual's defensive constellation and its expression, on the other. Farnfield's subtitle "Or … What has attachment theory ever done for us?" hints at a recognition of this tension and the impossibility, or indeed undesirability, of resolving it on one side or the other.

Building on Pat Crittenden's developmental theory and longitudinal research of mother–infant dyads from birth onwards, Farnfield explores the spectrum of preoccupied attachment, or Type C, strategies. He describes how Type C is elaborated from infancy and how, as different capacities mature, there may be greater emphasis on either anger or helplessness as the primary defensive strategy. He also describes the role of trauma in damaging sequencing, as evidenced by the Adult Attachment Interview, a finding that calls to mind a developing object relations perspective on "narrative skin" and the need for "narrative repair" with borderline patients rather than, or at any event prior to, interpretive intervention (Turp, 2012).

Farnfield demonstrates that the extreme end of the spectrum denotes severe disturbance of the kind associated with personality disorder and psychosis: "By C7–8, comfort is deemed impossible and overtures of reassurance and nurture, from a therapist or others, may be misconstrued as covert attempts to mislead the subject into believing he is safe in order to abuse him." The persecutory fantasies alluded to call to mind the torments described by Amanda Jones in her account of mother Sarah and her imagined persecution by her child Maisie. Particularly striking (and particularly helpful for those of us not versed in interpreting figures and diagrams) are the cited extracts from Farnfield's research. The chilling extracts from interviews with Griff, age four; Wesley, age sixteen; and Tony, age forty-five, leave us in no doubt with regard to the relevance of this research to understanding violence and criminality. Without directly alluding to either parent–infant psychotherapy or other clinical work, Farnfield's paper underlines the importance of such research and the potential personal and social consequences of leaving therapeutic needs unmet—consequences he no doubt encountered in his previous career in social work.

Beyond this, the model he constructs with both care and precision offers an invaluable framework for thinking in depth about the nature and severity of attachment disturbance, as its contours reveal themselves in the context of the therapeutic encounter.

* * *

Anne Power's chapter is a fitting end to the book, thoughtfully elaborating ideas previously referred to and bringing an additional perspective from the point of view of transactional analysis. A particular strength of Power's contribution is her refreshingly honest account of countertransference pitfalls, with particular reference to the difficulty in sustaining empathy in the face of self-defeating defensive strategies. "Like a traveller who never finds their destination, or a hungry person who does find food but is unable to swallow, they have the experience of being destined to seek help from which they can never benefit." Power attributes countertransference difficulties in part to the oscillation of "display"/ "racket" and "authentic" feelings in the preoccupied patient, with the therapist always in danger of being in thrall to the "stage direction" of the display feelings and entering into an enactment. While the categories of "racket" and "authentic" feelings originate in transactional analysis, there are links here to Crittenden's work on coercive aggression and coercive feigned helplessness, and thus to the research undertaken and described by Farnfield. In common with both Cundy and Jones, Power is much concerned with the problem of mourning and devotes a section of her chapter to chronic and complicated grief, drawing on the Kleinian literature to deepen her own and our understanding.

Power's perspective on the question of categorisation includes her particular interest in "mixed patterns", for example children who are strongly dismissing with one parent and preoccupied with the other, and in the interaction between the setting in the home (or boarding school) and the way in which an attachment pattern manifests. Drawing together various strands of thought, she offers the following conclusion:

> We have spent a day reflecting on work with people who manage themselves and others with preoccupied strategies, and I think this has indicated how helpful it can be to recognise a client's predominant way of relating, but I think we would say it is not necessary. There will be cases where we cannot discern a predominant pattern and perhaps the value of the question then is not the answer but the process of enquiry which may sharpen our curiosity and deepen our commitment to understanding and reaching this person.

* * *

In this small volume, we encounter a range of insights into a mode of relating that most of us will recognise from our therapeutic encounters. Each of the contributors offers a particular perspective on the task of applying attachment-based and psychoanalytic research in the service of detailed description of preoccupied attachment and the predisposing and protective factors associated with it. Each of them testifies to the personal commitment and intensive training undertaken by attachment-based and psychoanalytic practitioners alike, such that they are able to retain a capacity to think when confronted with the—at times extreme—pressures unconsciously exerted on the therapist by the preoccupied patient. We are indebted to the contributors, and to Linda Cundy who curated the conference, for their enhancement of our understanding, an understanding crucial to our capacity to enable the recovery of those who have perforce adopted a preoccupied attachment style early in life—a style that at one time operated in the service of survival and now thwarts and compromises their attempts at relationship at every turn.

References

Crittenden, P. (2000). Attachment and psychopathology. In: S. Goldberg, R. Muir, & J. Kerr (Eds.), *Attachment Theory: Social, Developmental, and Clinical Perspectives* (pp. 367–406). Hillsdale, NJ: Analytic Press.

Fonagy, P. (2001). *Attachment Theory and Psychoanalysis*. New York: Other Press.

Robertson, J., & Robertson, J. (1971). Young children in brief separation: a fresh look. *Psychoanalytic Study of the Child, 26*: 264–315.

Turp, M. D. (2012). Clinging on for dear life: adhesive identification and experience in the countertransference. *British Journal of Psychotherapy, 28*: 66–80.

CHAPTER ONE

Fear of abandonment and angry protest: understanding and working with anxiously attached clients

Linda Cundy

O ur attachment patterns lay the foundations of unconscious beliefs about ourselves, and expectations we hold of other people and relationships. These belief systems are played out in the therapeutic relationship, influencing transference and countertransference, attitudes to boundaries, and how the therapy is used. This presentation focuses on individual therapy with adults, outlining what preoccupied attachment looks like in general and in the consulting room, highlighting difficulties that commonly arise in therapy, and proposing aims and a specific focus for therapeutic work with preoccupied clients.

Of course, in trying to better understand our clients, we may also recognise ourselves in the descriptions that follow. It is a natural progression, a creative use of talents, for a compulsive caregiver to train in and practise counselling or psychotherapy. If you do identify as "anxiously attached", then I hope your own therapy has enabled you to stand back and observe the processes I describe without being overwhelmed by feelings too often. Therapeutic work with clients who are insecure and tormented by memories that continually fuel anger and helplessness quite frequently gets stuck or even ends badly. Certainly, I find these the most challenging clients, the ones I take to supervision most often.

1

However, when practitioners can identify the core difficulties and dynamics and adjust their interventions accordingly, there is real cause for hope—as many here today may testify.

More than half of patients in my private practice struggle with this particular pattern of attachment, and I suspect that they are over-represented in mental health services, voluntary sector counselling services, and the Improving Access to Psychological Therapies (IAPT) scheme, compared to those with an avoidant/dismissive pattern of relating. This is regardless of the fact that twenty-five per cent of the population in Britain is estimated to be dismissing, compared to just eleven to fifteen per cent enmeshed/preoccupied (the figure varies according to research project). However, findings from the Adult Attachment Interview (AAI) suggest that a further ten per cent show evidence of being unresolved in respect of trauma or loss. The interview transcripts from this latter group indicate a basic attachment pattern that could be secure, dismissing, or preoccupied but their language breaks down in response to particular questions, indicating unintegrated thoughts and defences against them. So individuals may combine preoccupied and unresolved qualities.

Where a mother–infant dyad is predominantly anxious–ambivalent but the child is exposed to repeated traumatic experiences such as parents fighting, domestic violence, physical or sexual abuse, then he is likely to develop particular patterns of relating to other people and to himself. This sets a trajectory towards the preoccupied/unresolved subcategory that we may know by another name. Peter Hobson and colleagues undertook research using the AAI to explore how early experiences affect and potentially disrupt the ability to think. All interviewees were women diagnosed either with chronic depression or borderline personality disorder. What they discovered was that *all* of those with a borderline personality disorder diagnosis "were enmeshed/preoccupied in their thinking about their early relationships" (Hobson, 2004, p. 158). Additionally, ten out of these twelve women were "confused, fearful and overwhelmed in relation to past experiences with significant figures. Therefore the women whose relationships were in turmoil and who often showed very troubled relationships with themselves (for example, cutting themselves or being self-destructive in other ways) … seemed haunted by something they could not resolve" (ibid.).

Unresolved trauma is not the focus of this presentation, but it may help us to understand our preoccupied clients when they appear almost borderline in response to a life crisis. They have very limited resources to help them process difficult events and are perhaps more easily traumatised than secure or dismissing individuals.

First, we need to recognise preoccupied patterns of attachment and appreciate something of the internal and interpersonal dynamics. For the sake of clarity, I will use the masculine pronoun when describing anxiously attached individuals and the feminine pronoun in relation to therapists.

Features of preoccupied attachment in adults

People are complex. With our evolutionary capacity to adapt to new environments, we can adjust ourselves in relation to other people. We may find ourselves feeling secure around a certain colleague but more dismissing, preoccupied, or even disorganised around others. We affect them in turn, bringing out different aspects of each other's interpersonal repertoires. This capacity to adjust ourselves in relation to the influences of others is essential in parenting and may be a vital component of therapeutic skill. Noticing how we are "used" by each client and our countertransference responses to subtle levels of communication form a core of technique in many therapeutic approaches. But when we are under sufficient duress, our core attachment patterns and defences emerge. As Steve Farnfield said, "all people have an underlying strategy".

Clearly, there is also spectrum of intensity when we look at this genre of anxious attachment. Some individuals manage to contain their anxieties most of the time, even appearing rather dismissing in their relationships with others—until there is a crisis that shatters these defences and reveals a core of preoccupation. Brooding and anger reveal a different defensive strategy aimed at preventing abandonment. I make sense of this by imagining an infant with a rather tantalising but inconsistent mother. The original pattern of attachment between them is ambivalent, and the child tries repeatedly to recapture and hold onto mother's love and attention. But eventually he gives up, accepting that he cannot rely on her for containment, comfort, or reassurance—he must learn to provide these for himself. And so he does, until a later relationship breaks down and he is confronted with the original yearning, love-hunger, and desperate need that he once felt for his mother.

Another possible scenario is the dyad where mother is loving and attentive but her anxiety is too invasive. Perhaps the child, once he has developed certain cognitive capacities, discovers methods for protecting himself and his integrity from her intrusions. But again, these more developmentally mature strategies can be shattered by loss or threat of it in later life, triggering a regressive return to the core attachment pattern. This often takes his family, his circle of friends, and the person himself by surprise—they do not recognise the person "he has become". Winnicott wrote about people who dread breaking down because they suffered the agony of ego disintegration early in life and thus developed desperate defences to protect themselves from returning to this terrifying disintegrated state (Winnicott, 1974). The people I am thinking of here have already experienced the terror of abandonment created by inconsistent caregiving, and have then constructed different layers of defence against a repeat of the original situation. Under certain circumstances, when current relationships echo the first anxiety-provoking attachment, secondary defence mechanisms (avoidance and dismissal of intimate relating) break down to expose the original raw anxieties and the clinging, demanding, primitive strategies to hold on to the other who is needed as protector.

At the other end of the spectrum, there is the "borderline borderline" presentation, where there is so little capacity to tolerate anxiety that dysregulation frequently threatens. We may not see the active attacks on the self (or others) that feature in borderline personality disorder, but we do see other more covert methods to undermine the self, as well as aggression towards others.

* * *

The unifying factors among this spectrum of self-experience are the core anxiety of being abandoned and patterns of defence aimed at preventing separation; all else stems from this. From childhood on, attachment-eliciting behaviours are resorted to in order to attract the care and attention of others and hold on to them once their attention has been captured. Coercive helplessness, angry protest, and even illness are found to be effective in preventing desertion. A further feature is the difficulty accessing space to think and reflect. As children, they "learned [to] emphasize affect and disregard, or defend against, cognition" (Crittenden, 2000, p. 382). This denies them a useful resource in life.

While the core anxiety and range of defensive strategies form a general pattern, each individual evolves in a specific relational environment and context, and every person's situation is influenced in subtle or not so subtle ways by a unique constellation of fantasies. In detailing the features of preoccupied attachment, I risk stereotyping. I prefer to think in terms of an archetype, a "pure form" containing an essence that we can recognise in different manifestations. For this reason, I introduce you to Archie. Archie is an archetype of anxious attachment whose qualities are distilled from many patients I have worked with (and people I have known personally).

Archie's internal world is filled with anxious fretting and grievance. To other people, his anger and distress seem disproportionate to the events he protests against. He is easily offended. His relationships are enmeshed and rather too claustrophobic for some friends, who find his need for their time and attention too demanding. When they pull back from him a little—perhaps not responding immediately to a phone call or text message—Archie panics. He is hypervigilant to signs of rejection. He may persist in his attempts to make contact, perhaps escalating the intensity of his communications, or he may withdraw angrily and contact another friend, engaging her with complaints about the offending person in long tirades. The implicit message is "don't you withdraw from me too, or I'll say bad things about you to others in our social group".

Archie can also be very caring. He likes to be helpful, though at times his generosity can feel intrusive and seems to imply an obligation to those being helped. He feels resentful when they appear to forget all he has done for them—"you would have thought they'd invite me after all I've done for them, wouldn't you?" Woe betides you if you do not agree with him on this point! Archie needs people whose minds are the same as his, and he struggles with different perspectives.

Along with compulsive caregiving, another strategy for getting his needs met is helplessness. After falling out with his friend, Archie is so upset that he collides his bicycle with a parked vehicle and breaks his arm in the resulting fall. He ensures that his cast is visible when meeting people in the street, but refuses any help offered by the friend whose unkind behaviour preceded the accident. As he clearly cannot manage to shop, cook, or get around with a broken arm, other people step in to help, and they may be required to take sides in what is turning into a feud.

Although Archie has fallen out with an old friend, that relationship dominates his thoughts and actions. His mind is so full of repetitive brooding, and he is so prone to intense emotions, that he has little internal space for reflection. He is more inclined to impulsive action than conscious choice. He continually fuels the conflict, punishing the person who has let him down. And what is curious here is the particular quality of his anger. Despite rejecting any advances his now ex-friend makes towards him, Archie keeps the grievance alive in his mind. This implies that he is not ready to bury the relationship. It is not yet the anger of despair or mourning. The two are bound together in a drama where bitterness has replaced love—but the attachment is just as alive, and perhaps more intense.

These are not particularly likable qualities, but we must remember that, for Archie, these strategies developed in childhood and were adopted because they worked for him; they were effective in ensuring the attentions of his specific attachment figures.

> The anxious stance ... is encouraged by (1) unreliable care, which is sometimes affectionate and at other times neglectful; (2) intrusive care that is more related to the caregiver's own needs and anxieties than to the needs of the attached individual; (3) care that discourages the acquisition of self-regulation skills and, directly or indirectly, punishes a person for attempting to function independently; (4) comments that emphasize a person's helplessness, incompetence, or weakness when trying to operate autonomously; and (5) traumatic or abusive experiences endured when one is separated from attachment figures.
>
> (Mikulincer, Shaver, Cassidy, & Berant, 2009, p. 297)

This kind of early environment discourages children from developing skills that would enable them to function autonomously. Anxious and inconsistent mothering makes children afraid to explore the world. They grow up needing other people to help them manage many aspects of their lives, and yet they also expect other people to be inconsistent and let them down. If we cannot guarantee that there is somebody always by our side as we negotiate life, we can at least ensure that there is always someone occupying every corner of our internal world. Archie is never alone as long as he rages against his one-time best friend.

"With exploration comes self-confidence and relative autonomy ... [this helps] the individual to make realistic judgments of his own strengths and limitations so that he will know when it is appropriate ...

to ask for help" (Parkes, 1982, p. 298). Archie never had the opportunity to internalise a secure base so was never able to take advantage of opportunities and challenges that might have helped him find better solutions to his dilemmas. He was not able to develop the resilience to recover from a narcissistic wound. He has never been able to stand back and see events from a different point of view, let alone consider whether he has misread his friend's intentions.

Having failed to firmly internalise secure experiences and "good objects", he lacks the internal resources for self-soothing, self-containment, or self-encouragement. Unable to gauge when it is appropriate to ask for help, Archie continues to make unreasonable demands of other people. But even when relational feeding is offered, he has difficulty taking it in, holding on to it, digesting and being nourished by it. These "secure attachment experiences" do not help him establish a secure base inside himself. Rather than internalising the care and attention he receives, he remains focused on what is missing.

The needs of Archie and others who are preoccupied seem insatiable, especially when their relationships are threatened. This can take the form of sibling rivalry when there is competition for limited resources, and an inconsistent attachment figure will certainly fuel these fears of deprivation when she must share herself between two or more children. Intense envy of the other who appears to be favoured, or who is "greedy" enough to get the lion's share of love and affection, can dominate sibling relationships throughout entire lives. Several of my clients appear haunted by envy of—and by—siblings that can be traced back to early childhood. In all cases, the mother's own limited resources and inconsistency are at the root of competition for her favours. I have also noted that, for some of these preoccupied patients, identifying a sibling as the "bad object" onto whom all resentment and blame are directed has effectively protected the mother from being contaminated by such destructive feelings. She has been kept pure, perfect, and longed-for in the minds of these individuals.

Archie, however, happens to be an only child and his feelings for his parents are much more ambivalent. Despite his rage against them for all their perceived failures, he still longs for their love, and much of his behaviour is intended to communicate his needs to them. But Archie's parents died many years ago. Like the friend who let him down, his parents are kept alive and kicking in his mind. In particular, he appears to have a complicated relationship with his (internal) mother. In reality, there were many times he can recall of intimacy, fun, and love with her when he was young, but she suffered from frequent bouts of depression, during which she took to her bed. Her small son tried to cheer her up and look after her, but sometimes this seemed to anger her, so she would shout at him and lock her door. It is not surprising that he developed quite different images of her—the loving, doting mother who made him feel special, the anxious, needy, depressed mother who over-compensated by being sentimental and infantilising her son, and the angry, rejecting mother who completely withdrew from him, leaving him terrified of what might happen. These multiple models are reminiscent of those held by toddlers in the Strange Situation Test who approach a parent for reassurance while effectively backing away from the same parent as if he or she is the source of the danger. For Archie, there was just enough consistency, not quite enough trauma to set the scene for psychopathology.

> Preoccupied attachment is associated with ... childhood experience of intrusive or role-reversing parenting in which the child's attention is persistently focused on a parent who is described as incompetent, ill, overconcerned, or unduly critical of the child. Such parent—child relationships appear to be highly involving, intensely conflictual, and often accompanied by confusing or contradictory communications. Such interactions may severely compromise the child's sense of self and autonomy of thought and action.
>
> (Adam, Sheldon Keller, & West, 2000, p. 332)

Archie struggles with intimate relationships. Quiet contentment is rarely available to him. He needs to feel intensely in order to feel real, and to feel that the relationship is real. He was besotted with his previous partner and very attentive—she might describe him as controlling—always thoughtful about gifts that would make her happy, meeting her from work each day to travel home with her. Hypersensitive to insult or rejection, he was suspicious and jealous of her contact with others. He checked her emails, text messages, and internet history when she started returning home late from work. When she packed her bags to leave him, Archie begged her to stay and implied that he would take an overdose if she gave up on him. He has "never got over her".

* * *

Of my preoccupied patients, many of those who occupy the more extreme end of the spectrum—the "borderline lite" end—have not been in a long-term romantic relationship for many years, even decades. They have discovered how dangerous and dysregulating intimate relationships can be for them and fear risking their equilibrium, even their sanity, by getting close to anyone again. This may seem inconsistent with the need for attachment and attention, the fear of being alone. While they appear to live rather solitary lives, their internal worlds are populated with the ghosts of parents, friends, and ex-lovers who are clung to obsessively, and actual relationships with real people in the real world are often conflictual enough to guarantee that they continue to exist in other peoples' minds. Arguing, provoking resentment, and blaming keep the heat turned up.

Despite maintaining a place in other peoples' minds, often through provocative behaviour, Archie has little faith in his own capacity to influence them. He doesn't expect to be taken seriously, yet he broods on what he perceives to be injustice, believing that others have what is denied to him. Curiously for a man who has such a tenuous sense of himself as an individual, he has a strong sense of entitlement. Having paid such close attention to his mother's needs, especially during her depressive episodes, perhaps he feels he is owed some care, or at least recognition for his efforts. He also has a keen feeling for justice and longs for acknowledgement that he has suffered and been wronged.

I understand this to reflect a defensive inflation of the ego, or self. Preoccupied individuals struggle to function autonomously or experience themselves as effective in their lives, but may feel more protected by adopting a kind of narcissistic grandiosity. This is often also at the expense of one or more other characters in their life story who are designated as "bad" and denigrated. Equally, unhappy events from the distant past are elevated to the status of outrages, defining moments in the creation of the self.

Further features of Archie's internal world include his difficulty letting go of grievances. Wrapped up in rumination over past events, he has little mental space for reflecting on the present or looking to the future.

Making sense of other peoples' minds helps us understand their motives and predict their behaviours, which in turn helps us make realistic judgements about threat, opportunity, action, and outcome. But for the preoccupied individual, maternal inconsistency and conflicting messages have left him vulnerable to misreading other peoples' intentions. If a neighbour is kind, he may judge it appropriate to ask her for help without considering the neighbour's own life—in other words, he may be unboundaried in his demands. Or he may wrongly interpret an email from his boss as critical and feel his hackles rise. His impulse may be to take offence and storm out of his new job. Thankfully, Archie realises that he needs to understand what makes people tick. He doesn't yet know it, but he lacks a coherent and realistic theory of mind.

Most of my anxiously attached clients become aware that they misunderstand other people and recognise that it would help them to have a meaningful framework to make sense of human behaviour and human minds. Many of them choose to study psychology, counselling, or psychotherapy. Others are drawn to different paradigms, including religions, pop psychology, new age philosophies, spiritual practices, or astrology. Whatever I personally feel about these choices, I do welcome the desire to find a model of what it is to be human. For me, an integration of attachment theory with object relations provides a structure for thinking about experiences that makes perfect sense.

I have become very fond of Archie (or, of all the patients whose stories have been attributed to him), but it took a lot of time and work to fully appreciate the deficits in his experience as a result of his history and the context in which he grew up. Without this perspective, I found him really hard-going. It also helped enormously to discover ways of making sense of his internal world that enabled me to be more effective as his psychotherapist.

Presentation in therapy

A distinctive feature of psychotherapy with preoccupied clients concerns boundaries. Anxiously attached clients may arrive early and often overstay session times. They often seek out contact between sessions, for instance sending updates on material discussed in the session, emailing photos of family events, forwarding wise words, images, or witty stories found online, or copying the therapist into emails. There is a sense that challenging such actions will be interpreted as rejection or criticism, with the therapist becoming a bad object for the client—so it is easier to allow these boundary anomalies to persist. In the early days of my private practice, I worked with a patient whom I found difficult to manage at the end of sessions. Despite my attempts to end on time, we frequently overran considerably, and even when I succeeded in drawing the session to a timely close, he still spent up to ten minutes "refreshing himself" in the bathroom. I have not seen him for many years, but his legacy lives on in the pattern of my appointments on Fridays, allowing an extra ten minutes between mid-morning sessions instigated to minimise the stress on myself and reduce the risk of him bumping into the next client.

Preoccupied clients often request a change of appointment time to facilitate other aspects of their lives, or ask for extra appointments on an *ad hoc* basis. Sometimes it suits them to have their therapy on the telephone or via video-conferencing rather than coming to the consulting room. There is a wish to be special, to be made an exception, to be fed on demand. But this is also a re-enactment of an unpredictable relationship with chaotic boundaries. The therapist is being manoeuvred into position to represent an enticing but ultimately disappointing parent.

Payment for private therapy can also present problems: it is painful to pay for somebody's care and attention, so invoices may be ignored and debts mount up. Attempts to address this can be interpreted as lack of trust in the patient's integrity or failure to appreciate the difficulties he is facing. Therapy may be angrily terminated, or the therapist punished in other ways.

Of course, the therapist's breaks are also a further cause for protest, dysregulating the client and inviting acting out or retaliation. However unpleasant it is to be on the receiving end of these attacks on our boundaries, we must understand them as attachment-eliciting behaviours that historically have proved successful for the patient. That does not mean we should acquiesce to coercion.

Preoccupied clients endeavour to create an intimate, intense relationship with the therapist by asking personal questions, bringing gifts, and being intrusive in other ways. Of course, we cannot expect new patients to know the rules of therapy, but dismissing individuals would never dream of taking such liberties. One patient demanded that I move my chair closer to his and was furious when I refused. He later visited my bathroom, where I heard him opening cupboards. I felt violated. It was one of those therapies that terminated before any useful work could be done.

I imagine we have all had the uncomfortable experience of being presented with a gift and knowing it is both unwise to accept it and unwise to refuse. Difficult though it is to reject the gesture and offend the giver, it is likely to undermine the work if the meaning and intention behind the gift cannot be thought about together.

* * *

Preoccupied individuals are more likely to seek therapy than those with dismissing attachment patterns because they are keenly aware of their need for other people to help them manage life's ups and downs. They may initially idealise the therapist but their unconscious expectation, based on their core internal working model, is that the therapist will ultimately let them down and abandon them. And of course, they use all the tactics available to them to push the boundaries and invite rejection. Our job is to hold the boundaries and link these feelings and behaviours to the past, where they originated.

A further difficulty in the work is due to these clients struggling to take in good experiences and incorporate them. We can find our sensitive empathic comments and carefully crafted interpretations rejected, especially after there has been an upset in therapy. Maggie Turp wrote of one patient "devouring my words voraciously while at the same time refusing to hear what I was saying" (2012, p. 70). Despite the hungry devouring, these clients so rarely feel nourished by what they consume.

Acting out is one form of communication to the therapist; leaving sessions early, forgetting appointments or payment, disappearing for a time and not responding to messages are all intended to be felt as rebukes and warnings. "If a person has not been helped with integrating strong feelings, then action may take the place of thinking" (Hobson, 2004, p. 175). Illness may also be a message to the therapist about distress or offence caused. A further form of acting out occurs when the patient engages in a therapy-like arrangement with somebody else. This may be a cognitive behavioural therapist recommended by the GP, a specialist dietician, psychic, astrologer, or online self-help community. This creates opportunities for splitting between the good, loving, ever-giving attachment figure and the inadequate, withholding, fragile, or angry attachment figure. It is more helpful for the patient to experience the therapist as someone who can usually be relied upon to be caring and helpful (within the fifty minutes of the session) but who occasionally falls short. The intention is what matters, and the patient's capacity to let go of disappointment or resentment because of lapses is a great developmental achievement.

Preoccupied individuals make intense transference relationships. They invest a great deal of importance in key figures in their lives, including their psychotherapists, perceiving them as both the longed-for, exciting ideal mother and the disappointing, ineffectual, infuriating "mother who fails". Because of their internal working models, they expect to get only nuggets of anything useful from the therapist.

A trap that we can easily fall into is when the client invites the therapist to offer advice (we may even offer this unsolicited at times). But whatever suggestions we make are bound for rejection before we finish uttering them. There is always a reason why our insights cannot possibly help. We have been effectively drawn into a re-enactment where we are cast as an ineffectual attachment figure, one that has nothing of use to offer, with no appreciation of how difficult life is for the client. But if we refrain from playing the game, we may be perceived as attachment figures who do have answers but who are heartlessly refusing to help. Perhaps you also recognise the situation where you have held your tongue when asked for advice then at a later session heard that "I did what you suggested"! Sometimes it seems that the advice the client believed we offered was helpful and other times not. But perhaps this is just an example of the confusion these patients, whose sense of their own individuality is so tenuous, can sometimes feel about where their minds end and other people's begin.

The material brought to therapy by the preoccupied client often takes the form of complaints about other peoples' cruelty or thoughtlessness. He fills all the space with unnecessary detail of events that may date back decades, and his skewed interpretation of them. The therapist is invited to collude in demonising the offending party and faces an angry reaction (often disguised, or passive aggressive, or even sulky) if she opts to refrain from making judgement. Emotions are often intense, and there may be frequent life dramas reported. These are not on the same scale of the crises experienced by clients with unresolved trauma, but all tend to highlight the patient's sense of being victimised or treated unfairly, and the failure of all his attempts to be effective. In other words, they are all repetitions of scenarios that dominate his thoughts from earlier in his life.

This material quickly becomes stale and frustrating, and the therapy feels stagnant, as if nothing can be changed. There is often little space in the session for thought or reflection. I discovered early on that some patients have a way of silencing me by ignoring anything I say or simply not allowing space for me to contribute anything, leaving me feeling helpless and hopeless. It is vital to find my voice early in each session, even if my contributions are rejected. At least I can then use my mind, see the dynamic in action, and comment on what I observe. The therapeutic venture must not be obliterated.

General aims of attachment-based therapy

It is unusual for a person whose attachment history is secure to seek therapy, so I assume that the great majority of clients begin with an insecure attachment pattern—preoccupied, dismissing, or unresolved in respect of trauma or loss. The aim is for the patient to develop ways of being with other people and with himself that indicate he has "earned" security. But what does this mean? And what needs to happen to bring about the transformation?

The practice of attachment-based psychotherapy places great emphasis on the healing value of mourning. All clients need to recognise and grieve for what they have lost that was important, and what they have been deprived of that is essential for healthy development. The therapist's task is to facilitate the client engaging with the mourning process, moving through it, and eventually looking to the future. If it happens to be a loved one who has died, a fairly straightforward bereavement, then the bereaved person must confront the reality of the loss and accept that his world has changed forever. Feeling and expressing the pain, sadness, and anger that are part of grieving, he can eventually let go of hope of reunion, discover his own resources, and reconstruct a life for himself in this changed environment. Other kinds of loss may seem intangible or too distant to be significant, and there are defences in place to prevent acknowledging the pain and damage done.

The internal working models that govern our perception of the world, of relationships, and of ourselves are organised around a core anxiety—that of being intruded on or being abandoned. The patterns of attachment that develop from these anxieties were functional in early life, they got results in terms of eliciting care and attention from our particular caregivers in their particular context when we were most dependent on them. However, these strategies for seeking connection with other people and protecting ourselves from them are not so effective in adult life. Another aim of therapy is to help clients modify their expectations of relationships, to explore new ways of relating to others, and to modify their original defences.

When a client recognises that he was denied experiences that are fundamental to happiness, self-esteem, and security, we hope that he can begin to feel compassion for himself as a child. Rather than continuing to deprive himself of good experiences, or tormenting himself with fears, or feeling crippling shame at his perceived inadequacies, we aim to help him transform his relationship with himself. In order to bring about such a radical change, he needs to internalise positive experiences with other people, including the therapist, to form the basis of a new "internal secure attachment object", a resource that can help to calm him when his anxiety is escalating, protect him from situations that could be dysregulating, encourage his efforts, delight in his successes, and forgive his failures.

A further task is to build the patient's emotional resilience, to help him be courageous, try new experiences, stand up for himself, make decisions, and recover more quickly from disappointments and setbacks. This is easier if he has a sense of his therapist not only supporting him and skilfully challenging him in the consulting room, but also becoming part of the personal resources he carries around with him every day. The patient gradually becomes his own therapist.

Specific aims of therapy with preoccupied clients

According to Holmes: "The overall goals of therapy can be summarized as the search for *intimacy* and *autonomy* [where] the capacity for intimacy arises out of attunement, while a sense of autonomy comes from the successful expression of healthy protest and, where loss is irretrievable, grieving" (2001, p. 49). These are capacities that secure individuals can take for granted. True "intimacy" requires two autonomous individuals who enjoy times of emotional closeness as well as time apart. Each has a mind of his or her own. For anxiously attached individuals, close relationships are often more enmeshed than truly intimate; they are most comfortable when the unit comprises two people whose needs, wishes, and ways of being are symbiotically tangled up. And for children whose attachment figures are unreliable, autonomy cannot develop. They need to stay focused on the parent, try to read his or her changing moods, and attend to the parent's needs in order to receive some scraps of security. If the caregiver was anxious, depressed, addicted, or simply overwhelmed, it was never safe to protest in the service of autonomy. Winnicott wrote about the child's need to attack and "destroy" the mother with whom he is symbiotically fused in order to establish himself as separate from her (1969). But this is not possible when mother is too frail or unstable to tolerate the attack. Later, as a preoccupied adult, angry protest is intended to keep the other engaged and involved rather than create a boundary between two autonomous individuals.

If the aim of attachment-based psychotherapy is greater security and autonomy, how do we help our preoccupied clients achieve this transformation? I have listed nine therapeutic aims specific to this client group below, and will elaborate on these later, as well as discussing the matter of mourning in greater detail.

1. Develop healthy affect regulation.
2. Create space for thought.
3. Establish firm interpersonal boundaries.
4. Promote self-awareness, the client's capacity to observe his thoughts, impulses, feelings, and behaviour.
5. Develop psychological-mindedness, a coherent model of minds.
6. Construct a meaningful narrative.
7. Build a stronger sense of self and agency.
8. Strengthen capacity for empathy and compassion for others.
9. Internalise a new "good object".

But let us start at the beginning of the therapy.

Assessment

Good therapy starts with a good assessment. As a private practitioner, I have the luxury of being able to take time with an assessment phase. That may not be possible for you in the settings you work in, but there is one thing that needs to be identified quickly—the client's core attachment pattern. And this is particularly important for preoccupied patients. By conducting an initial meeting that is semi-structured, letting the patient take the lead but interjecting with questions based on the AAI (see Farnfield, Chapter Three) at appropriate opportunities, it is possible to collect information from a number of sources to enable a hunch to be formulated. This may, of course, be revised as therapy continues, but I find it enormously helpful to make a formulation at the start.

When the client talks about past or present relationships, whether spontaneously or in response to a specific question, I try to listen to the form of his language as well as the content. How much detail does he provide? How much seems relevant and how much appears obsessive? How much of his speech is devoted to emotions rather than reflection? How much time does he take up in the session with talking rather than listening or asking questions? Do I feel talked *at* rather than talked to?

I try to note how he presents himself and other people in his life. Is everything he brings to the session about relationships with other people, or do they hardly figure in his thoughts at all? How persecuted does the client appear to be by people in his life? To what extent does he idealise or demonise others or himself?

I also pay attention to his attitude to boundaries. Does he phone in a panic on the day of the appointment? Arrive early, on time, or late? Overstay the allotted time? Does he bring someone with him and perhaps ask if the companion can sit in? Does he ask to record sessions on his mobile phone? Is there confusion around paying for the session, and does this contribute to the session ending late?

A further consideration is how a new client engages with me. Does he ask personal questions or seem completely uninterested in me? Does he relate to me as if I am an expert to be consulted? Or does he ignore my input and talk over me? Do I feel interviewed for a vacant post, or does the patient appear to accept me without reservation, almost indiscriminately?

There is one more source of information I take seriously—my countertransference. If I feel I have become an interrogator trying to extract information, then the client is unlikely to be preoccupied. If, on the other hand, I feel rather overwhelmed, suffocated, slightly frustrated, either irritated or helpless, and intruded upon, then my initial hunch (if backed up by the other sources of information) is likely to be "preoccupied".

There are important clinical implications of making a formulation as soon as possible, especially with individuals who need consistency but seem to unconsciously create situations of inconsistency and muddled boundaries. With these patients, boundaries should be explicit and, once agreed, the therapist must hold them steadfastly. The start of a therapy is an ideal opportunity for a re-enactment, with the client requesting a change of appointment time, engaging the therapist between session times, and so on. It may be necessary early in the therapy to explain that these therapeutic rules are important because they provide reliable structure for someone who probably lacked such predictable containment in early life.

The problem of mourning

John Bowlby recognised the importance of mourning in the healing of psychic pain. It is a process of accommodation to a new reality, accepting the permanence of loss. In giving up hope of reunion, we also let go of anger "in the service of attachment", the kind of behaviour we see when small children are temporarily separated from their parents. Their angry protest is intended to ensure that the adults pay closer attention in future to prevent a repeat of the frightening situation. Behind the anger in mourning, we find other painful feelings: sadness, fear, loneliness, confusion, and grief. These emotions, and the memories attached to them, need to be experienced fully before the loved one can be psychically laid to rest, or at least "relocated" in the internal world. Eventually, the bereaved individual is able to reconstruct his life and identity. He is ready to re-engage with the world, to reconnect with people, risk new relationships, and find pleasure in living once more.

Mourning is a transformative process that dissolves some of the certainties, the familiar ways of being. Through the experience of loss, internal working models can be reformulated. This provides a great opportunity for therapeutic intervention, but mourning is a painful experience, and many people defend against it. While some resist it entirely, others—as we shall see—resist moving through it to a transformative conclusion. "If the other person dies or leaves, a pathological mourning may be initiated whereby the person feels compelled to maintain a live picture of the other, in order to shore up the integrity of the self" (Fonagy & Target, 1998, p. 26).

* * *

Colin Murray Parkes, a colleague of Bowlby, outlined four phases of typical bereavement (Parkes, 1972). These are not necessarily experienced sequentially—the adjustment to reality is challenging and sometimes messy. The phases he identified are initial numbness, then a phase of yearning, pining, and searching for who (or what) has been lost. This is also the stage when the bereaved person may direct anger at whoever has died and left him, or misdirect it onto others. Eventually, as the reality is recognised, the individual is likely to sink into a depression, becoming disorganised and despairing. But ultimately, he is able to reorganise, perhaps to reinvent himself and create a new life for himself.

Aside from actual bereavement, what has been lost for the person who is anxiously attached is the consistent, reliable sense of security, of being special to those who were most important to him. He had a tantalising taste of love and safety but could not hold on to it, so he devotes the rest of his life to protesting about losing those precious times. But the very act of protest indicates that he is still trying to persuade his attachment figures to love him unconditionally. This is the tyranny of hope: he cannot, will not accept that it is too late, or that his attachment figures are simply not capable of giving him what he craves—their consistent support, encouragement, and belief in him.

Another model for thinking about loss, one that is particularly helpful for therapists, is that of Worden (1991). Again, he recognises that we move backwards and forwards through four phases, but he frames the process as a series of psychic tasks to be accomplished. The first of these is to accept the reality of loss. The next is to work through the pain of grief, then gradually to adjust to life without the deceased (or what has been lost, or never possessed). The final challenge is to emotionally relocate the deceased and move on, and this entails finding a new perspective on the past.

Again, we see that our preoccupied clients have not got beyond first base. Their anger is more grievance than grieving. It is a defence against feeling the pain, fear, and despair of grief. Their protest is unproductive, maintaining enmeshed relationships with "ghosts". It is the work of therapy to mobilise mourning, to undo resistance, and enable our preoccupied clients to give up hope.

"We'll have difficulties in mourning not because we loved someone too much, as common sense might suggest, but because our hatred was so powerful" (Leader, 2008, p. 48). Or our rage, or envy.

It is particularly problematic for a preoccupied person to give up on a relationship with someone who may still be living, for instance following marriage breakdown and divorce. For someone who is anxiously attached, it becomes necessary to demonise and hate in order to separate, but hatred and bitterness prevent the other from being emotionally relocated to a less significant position in the internal world. He or she continues to occupy the place of honour for many years. The internet, social networking, email, and text messaging provide so many ways to perpetuate destructive contact. There is an oft-repeated quote attributed to St Augustine of Hippo about resentment being "like taking poison

and expecting the other person to die". For many people, it is resentment that continues to breathe life into relationships that are effectively
long dead.

Leader notes that: "Killing the dead is a way of loosening one's bonds
to them and situating them in a different, symbolic space. It may then
become possible to start to forge new ties to the living, but this will
always follow a course specific to each individual" (ibid., p. 124). While
he points out that one aspect of "killing the dead" is to undo idealisa-
tion, for the clients we have in mind, it may be equally necessary to
undo the total denigration of people who were once loved.

The therapist's task is to encourage the mourning process to move
beyond the stage of protest, to facilitate the patient confronting the pain,
sadness, and loneliness hidden behind his anger.

I now return to the aims I outlined above as a focus for the work.
In reality, they are not separate but related; improvements in one area
will affect others, so I will consider some of them together.

Develop healthy affect regulation and create space for thought

Preoccupied individuals are "high reactors" to stress (Gerhardt, 2004).
As infants, their experience was of attachment figures who were poor
at regulating the child's emotional and physiological states. As a result,
their base levels of the stress hormone cortisol are relatively high. On top
of this, as children, they needed to exaggerate emotions such as anger,
fear, or distress in order to reach a caregiver who might otherwise not
respond. Intense feelings are the hallmark of this pattern of attachment,
along with difficulty regulating hyper-aroused states. In particular, they
struggle to disengage from negative affect (Nelson, 2009).

There are many techniques available to help clients down-regulate
highly charged emotional states, including meditation and mindful-
ness, art therapy, physical exercise, and writing. We aim to help our
preoccupied patients develop the internal resources to self-soothe, to
talk themselves down from escalating emotion, or to break the cycle of
brooding on specific events. This is part of creating space for thought,
and an opportunity to internalise the functions of the therapist.

Establish firm interpersonal boundaries

Preoccupied individuals are frequently unsettled by contact with certain people; every communication seems to stoke distress and lead to an

escalation of conflict. Sometimes the other person is genuinely intrusive and provocative, and the two are bound together in a kind of *folie à deux*. And sometimes it is the client's perception that the other person is selfish, envious, greedy, disrespectful, or manipulative, a perception distorted by transference, projection, and his internal working models. Either way, it is helpful to limit the contact. This may involve seeing less of the other person, revealing less to her, or even cutting contact altogether. Until there is some distance, it is not possible for the client to determine the real nature of the relationship.

We often see a conscious decision to limit, or even terminate contact, and an unconscious compulsion to re-engage. There is an addictive quality to these kinds of relationships, with all the therapeutic difficulties of working with addiction. It may be a case of "one day at a time" until progress has been made in other areas, such as the client becoming more self-aware and having more control over impulses. But ultimately, the capacity for true intimacy and autonomy, the achievement of earned security, will only be possible if he feels held by his own boundaries, able to choose what he shares with others, how much of himself to give, and when to say no.

One client cut contact with his brother for several years while we thought about the nature of their relationship in therapy. As he gained greater understanding of the dynamic between them and how this had evolved in the context of their family, he became able to think about the future and what he wanted from the relationship. He recognised that his previous demands for an apology had only inflated the conflict. With a more realistic understanding of his brother's personality, he was able to be tactical in his approaches, more psychological, and communicate in ways that improved his chances of getting his needs met.

In learning to contain his impulses, value the privacy of his mind, and be selective about what to share with whom, the preoccupied client adopts some of the characteristics that typify people with a dismissing pattern of attachment.

Therapeutic boundaries are essential in providing an atmosphere of safety and respect. The patient reveals his story to the therapist in manageable episodes to be processed together. He then practises containing himself until the next session, and the therapist's breaks provide opportunities to extend his new-found capacity to hold experiences inside himself until her return. This becomes easier as he begins to internalise the therapist, taking her functions into himself.

Promote self-awareness

The preoccupied client lacks a well-developed part of the self that stands back and observes his own reactions to events, the rise and fall of particular emotions, shifting body states, emerging thoughts and memories, impulses and behaviour. It is an important foundation for psychotherapy to enable such an observing ego to develop. By distancing himself a little from the drama, he can consider the connections between the trigger event, what happens in his internal world, and his impulse to action. He has the opportunity to choose a different response and to experience others responding differently to him. Impulse control can be achieved, minimising the fallout from escalating conflict.

You will remember that people who are chronically anxiously attached produce more stress hormones. "High cortisol levels are … associated with a highly active right brain and an underactive left brain" (Gerhardt, 2004, p. 121). Developing an observing ego involves activating left-brain capacities and also aids engagement of other brain regions. Rather than the event leading to immediate reflex action, perceptions of the event are processed, engaging the hippocampus and the prefrontal cortex. As well as inhibiting impulsive action, these brain regions are involved in organising narrative memory, with further constructive consequences.

The ability to stand back and observe oneself, and to make connections between current events, feelings, and past experiences, provides containment. Josephine Klein writes of "holding by ego-functioning" as a process that holds the personality together and strengthens sense of self—essential for the preoccupied person whose identity relies so much on other people. She lists "putting into words, combining concepts or ideas, remembering, reflecting upon, making connections between, making sense of, understanding the meaning of …" as components of self-containment (J. Klein, 1995, p. 85).

Once this capacity has developed in therapy, it becomes possible to link various domains of experience. It also enables the client to consider his deeper motives for behaviour.

A patient recently noted with great insight that "Part of me wants her right out of my head forever, but I know I'm not ready to kill her off yet. I still feel a sense of connection to her that I've never had with anyone else." This recognition gave us a really useful way to think about his internal conflict. In simultaneously wanting to let go of a past relationship and yet keep it alive, he had stumbled upon two relational models of himself with his mother—the person who initially loved him and filled his life with excitement, making him feel alive and special, and the person who could not be relied upon, who humiliated him, ignored his pain, and put her own interests first, making him feel worthless, bitter, and depressed. Following this session, I noted a qualitative change in him. His mood was lighter, he took a renewed interest in his appearance, and began to look to the future. Though not yet ready to consider another relationship, he seemed more oriented to hope. I was reminded of the Victorian custom of widows wearing matt black clothing following bereavement, leading to half-mourning of dark greys, then quarter-mourning, until it was considered respectable to move on.

Construct a meaningful narrative and build a stronger sense of self and agency

In the AAI, interviewees whose narrative style is overly detailed, featuring vocabulary biased towards emotion rather than thought, and who show evidence of being rather fixated with specific memories and relationships, are coded preoccupied. There is little evidence of considering the context or bigger picture. In order to "earn" security, the preoccupied client needs to turn his thoughts to that bigger picture in order to define himself within his own relational, social, cultural, and historical context.

This is the arena of storytelling, or at least of story-creating. I encourage patients to think about their family origins and, if possible, discover more. Social and historical events create ripples through the generations and give every family a unique identity. Just as the cultures of indigenous peoples are shaped by their creation myths, so each family is organised in subtle or explicit ways by the stories of previous generations—even when these stories are hushed up and forgotten.

By considering how wars and revolutions, famine, long traditions of farming or mining, poverty or wealth, education, opportunity, or tragedy shaped the client's prehistory and the relational environment he was born into, we help him consolidate his sense of identity and belonging. Of course, we cannot be sure of the historical accuracy of these stories, just as we cannot attest to the truthfulness of reconstructed events from childhood. They are a kind of postmodern truth—they are congruent with the available facts, and they help to make sense of experience, but need to be held lightly. Having a sense of the past and its continuing influence on the present, the client's sense of self is consolidated, and he can be freed up to turn his attentions to the future.

I am also interested in the patient's relationship to his cultural and religious origins, to his sexuality and gender. Exploring these areas again confirms his sense of who he is, where he fits in the world, what he chooses to hold on to from his upbringing, and what he prefers to redefine.

Develop psychological mindedness

> Through her mind I learned about my mind.
>
> (Zdrale, 2014, unpublished)

Someone who is psychologically minded is able to recognise that people behave as they do because they are influenced by certain needs, beliefs, feelings, thoughts, memories, and desires, and that these may be conscious or unconscious. This knowledge enables him to reflect on the influence of his own internal world on his behaviour. This is referred to as the capacity to mentalize, and is found in the AAI transcripts of people who are rated "secure", but is not significantly evident in those rated "insecure".

Insecurely attached people, including those who are preoccupied, lack a realistic or coherent model for making sense of other peoples' behaviour. As a result, they may misinterpret intentions, for instance by believing that a colleague who does not greet them with a smile is being disrespectful and contemptuous. They do not stop to consider their colleague's situation and make sense of the behaviour by connecting it with a recently diagnosed illness or heavy workload.

A vital aspect of effective therapy is helping the client understand how minds work. Having developed the ability to observe his own internal world and connect this to current and past events, he can be encouraged to recognise that other people also have experiences that motivate them.

In the AAI, one question in particular highlights the presence or absence of theory of mind: "Why do you think your parents behaved as they did?" Being able to view parents as having fantasies, motivations, abilities, and disadvantages as a result of their own histories, seeing them as people in their own right who existed before the client was even conceived, is enormously helpful.

During therapy, I explore these kinds of questions with patients. I ask why each parent may have behaved as they did. I ask what the client imagines were his parents' fantasies about him, what they wanted and needed from him, and where these wishes originated. What factors in their own lives may have influenced the kind of parenting they provided? How were their histories repeated in the relationships with him? What did they give him that they didn't have themselves as children?

Recognising that the people who created and raised him were shaped by their own experiences and the contexts of their lives helps him make sense of their limitations as parents. It is a reality that must be accepted. It is pointless to continue raging or clinging. This is not necessarily about forgiveness but about letting go. With acceptance, it may become possible to remember and appreciate some good things that were available in these relationships. After all, the rage is a protest about good things that were experienced then lost. Kleinians would refer to this as the achievement of the depressive position.

The absence of mentalization reflects the parents' inability to provide necessary conditions for theory of mind to grow. We need to create those conditions in therapy. Our interventions must be underpinned by a coherent theoretical model. Believing that there are reasons for feelings and behaviours, we set about discovering what these may be in the certainty that making sense of such mysteries is valuable.

But more than that, we need to communicate our own ability to mentalize by revealing our thought processes to the client. It is not necessary for him to know where we take our holidays or other personal details, but it is vital that he discovers how we make sense of the world. We need to find ways of sharing our minds with clients. "I have a theory about this—what do you think?" "When people tell me about x, I often wonder about y ..." "This may not make sense to you but humour me—let's consider the possibility that ..." And "what do you imagine I would say about this?"

Here is an extract from an email sent to me by a patient I have worked with for many years. I include it not out of vanity but because she expresses so vividly the relief that comes with having a theory of mind: "Your words mean so much to me. Sometimes I envy you with your abundant knowledge of the secrets of the mind and unconscious.

You shed light in grey places. It's helped me to learn about me and my world and the greater world about me. Nothing feels as good as that."

Psychologically minded parents are able to provide the context for their children to learn about minds: in other words, they are more likely to have children who are securely attached. "Mentalization may circumvent the need to repeat our own past in our relationships with our children" (Fonagy et al., 2000, p. 251). And importantly: "The association between parental reflective function and child security is strongest when there is adversity in the mother's history" (Bateman & Fonagy, 2004, p. 76). Earning security confers some advantages over those who have always taken it for granted.

Strengthen the capacity for empathy and compassion for others

In Graham Music's excellent book *The Good Life*, he traces connections between attachment security, empathy, and altruism (Music, 2014). He argues that we are born with innate tendencies towards morality, but how this develops depends on relationships with caregivers in early life. Reviewing considerable research, he notes that even very young children are capable of genuine acts of generosity, but it is the securely attached ones who demonstrate kindness and empathy more frequently. Being secure in themselves, they are able to imaginatively identify with others; taking for granted that they are loved, they can be interested in other people without feeling threatened, and can feel for them when they are unhappy. Secure adults give more to charity than do insecure ones, and show more pro-social concerns and behaviours.

Of ambivalently attached children, he notes that they can be sensitive to the moods of others, especially parents, but that this is not evidence of true empathy. Their attention is focused on how and when to approach their attachment figures, their anxiety levels are frequently high, and these are not the optimal requirements for empathy or real concern for others to flourish.

In order for our preoccupied client to achieve security, he needs to not only understand the minds of others but also to care about them. Establishing a secure base inside himself, supported by a new "good object", he has more mental and emotional availability for genuine relating. We cannot hurry or direct this development, but we can recognise when it begins to happen and delight in the different kind of responses he receives when he acts from this stronger position.

One patient who often feels invaded by her very intrusive mother spent most of a session complaining about unrealistic demands being made of her. Eventually, she was able to let me speak, and I pointed out that I understand how important it is for her to be a better mother than her own, and how much she respects her own child's autonomy. I assured her that she has control of her life and nobody has the right to coerce her or manipulate her choices. I encouraged her to protect herself from the pressure her mother continues to exert on her. I then wondered whether her mother envied her the life she has made for herself against all the odds. After letting my words sink in, she replied: "You're right. My poor Mum didn't have my opportunities. She would have loved to have an education but it just wasn't possible. There was no-one to support her."

With the development of empathy, it becomes more possible to consider the effect we have on other people. We might recognise occasions when we have been cruel, intending our words or actions to wound the other. We may even be able to reflect on times when our conscious intentions appear innocent but there has been a deeper, unconscious desire to hurt or punish. The therapist must find ways of challenging the simplistic story and open up an exploration of unconscious motives. "You are telling me x, but let's just consider the possibility that there was more to it than that. Let's just play with the idea that you may have been motivated by y …"

Internalise a new "good object"

It is easier to internalise an experience that is repeated and predictable. This again highlights the importance of firm therapeutic boundaries. The routine of relating during fifty- (or sixty-) minute therapy sessions, with all the rituals that evolve over time, helps the preoccupied client hold on to memories between appointments and when the therapy eventually ends. He is able to summon up the image of his psychotherapist, hear her voice in his mind, picture her expression and gestures, and remember her interventions—those that stand out for him as important and also the background generic ones. Then, when needed, he can call upon this new internal resource to calm and contain himself, to help him observe his feelings, impulses, and motives before acting, to create thinking space, and to challenge himself.

I encourage patients to reflect on "What would Linda think about this? What would she say?", and to report back. Once the therapy is well established, I may ask in the session "What question do you reckon I have in my mind?"

I also provide evidence of holding the client in mind, between sessions and over the course of therapy. I do not follow Bion's recommendation that we act "without memory or desire" (1967). I believe it is essential that preoccupied clients know they exist in our minds without needing to create a drama to ensure they are thought about. I also believe it is helpful to reflect on the history that is created between the two of us. "I remember you telling me a similar dream before"; "I seem to remember you really struggled this time last year too"; "Do you remember when we first met? I asked you why you thought you are an only child. Do you remember your answer?"

Anxiously attached individuals are afraid of abandonment. Having to manage alone is unthinkable, so it is preferable to cling to bad objects. Winnicott pointed out that we are never truly alone if we have good objects populating our internal worlds (1958). They are a resource to converse with and call upon. They enable us to act autonomously.

Resistance and self-sabotage

Preoccupied patients can be very resistant to change. Understanding the fear behind the resistance can enhance our empathy and guide our interventions.

One major obstacle concerns the quality of grievance. Our client may be trying to communicate to his attachment figures, even those who are no longer alive, "I will *not* give you the pleasure of seeing me thrive"; "Look how damaged I am. It is *your* fault, and *you* should provide restitution." The sense of injustice can be powerful, and it is painful to recognise that those who let them down could not have done better given their own difficulties.

Another form of this self-sabotage reflects unrequited longing: "If you see how much I suffer, you may change your mind and love me again." I have come across this often when romantic relationships come to an end.

For the ambivalently attached child, any attention from parents is better than none. The deepest fear is of ceasing to exist if he is not in the minds of other people, so he continues to make demands, provoke, or coerce others into responding. He may be afraid that they will choose to cut off from him if he gives them the opportunity, and he will be discarded, forgotten, and alone.

Finally, I have suggested that preoccupied individuals are "stuck" at an early stage of mourning, that they resist accepting the reality of loss with all that entails. By continuing to suffer and protest, our patient avoids feeling the despair that grieving entails. It is better to be angry than depressed—anger and pain can help him feel alive when he so fears losing others and himself.

Conclusion

As practitioners, we may find clients who are needy, demanding, angry, and seem resistant to benefiting from our help frustrating to work with. We may feel suffocated, criticised, or silenced in sessions and struggle to maintain our therapeutic stance. I have lost a number of preoccupied patients because I did not fully appreciate the depth of their distress, or because I lost hope. But if we can truly grasp the core anxiety and defences against it, there is hope that we can be effective, that we can help in the transformation from anxious attachment to earned security.

References

Adam, K. S., Sheldon Keller, A. E., & West, M. (2000). Attachment organization and vulnerability to loss, separation, and abuse in disturbed adolescents. In: S. Goldberg, R. Muir, & J. Kerr (Eds.). *Attachment Theory: Social, Developmental, and Clinical Perspectives* (pp. 309–341). Hillsdale, NJ: Analytic Press.

Bateman, A., & Fonagy, P. (2004). *Psychotherapy for Borderline Personality Disorder: Mentalization-Based Treatment.* Oxford: Oxford University Press.

Bion, W. R. (1967). Notes on memory and desire. *The Psychoanalytic Forum*, 2(3).

Crittenden, P. (2000). Attachment and psychopathology. In: S. Goldberg, R. Muir, & J. Kerr (Eds.), *Attachment Theory: Social, Developmental, and Clinical Perspectives* (pp. 367–406). Hillsdale, NJ: Analytic Press.

Fonagy, P., & Target, M. (1998). An interpersonal view of the infant. In: A. Hurry (Ed.), *Psychoanalysis and Developmental Therapy* (pp. 32–73). London: Karnac.

Fonagy, P., Steele, M., Steele, H., Leigh, T., Kennedy, R., Mattoon, G., & Target, M. (2000). Attachment, the reflective self, and borderline states: the predictive specificity of the Adult Attachment Interview and pathological emotional development. In: S. Goldberg, R. Muir, & J. Kerr (Eds.), *Attachment Theory: Social, Developmental, and Clinical Perspectives* (pp. 233–278). Hillsdale, NJ: Analytic Press.

Gerhardt, S. (2004). *Why Love Matters: How Affection Shapes a Baby's Brain.* Hove: Brunner-Routledge.

Hobson, P. (2004). *The Cradle of Thought: Exploring the Origins of Thinking.* Oxford: Oxford University Press.

Holmes, J. (2001). *The Search for the Secure Base: Attachment Theory and Psychotherapy.* Hove: Brunner-Routledge.

Klein, J. (1995). *Doubts and Certainties in the Practice of Psychotherapy.* London: Karnac.

Leader, D. (2008). *The New Black: Mourning, Melancholia and Depression.* London: Hamish Hamilton.

Mikulincer, M., Shaver, P. R., Cassidy, J., & Berant, E. (2009). Attachment-related defensive processes. In: J. H. Obegi & E. Berant (Eds.), *Attachment Theory and Research in Clinical Work with Adults* (pp. 328–347). New York: Guilford Press.

Music, G. (2014). *The Good Life: Wellbeing and the New Science of Altruism, Selfishness and Immorality.* London: Routledge.

Nelson, J. K. (2009). An attachment perspective on crying in psychotherapy. In: J. H. Obegi & E. Berant (Eds.), *Attachment Theory and Research in Clinical Work with Adults* (pp. 293–327). New York: Guilford Press.

Parkes, C. M. (1972). *Bereavement: Studies of Grief in Adult Life.* London: Tavistock.

Turp, M. (2012). Clinging on for dear life: adhesive identification and experience in the countertransference. *British Journal of Psychotherapy, 28*: 66–80.

Winnicott, D. W. (1958). The capacity to be alone. In: *The Maturational Processes and the Facilitating Environment* (pp. 29–36). London: Karnac, 1990.

Winnicott, D. W. (1969). The use of an object and relating through identifications. *International Journal of Psycho-Analysis, 50*: 711. [Reprinted in *Playing and Reality*. London: Tavistock, 1971.]

Winnicott, D. W. (1974). Fear of breakdown. *International Review of Psycho-Analysis, 1*: 103–107.

Worden, J. W. (1991). *Grief Counselling and Grief Therapy: A Handbook for the Mental Health Practitioner.* New York: Springer.

Zdrale, B. (2014). Personal project, submitted for the postgraduate diploma in attachment-based therapy, Wimbledon Guild (unpublished).

CHAPTER TWO

Softening a mother's need to reject her baby's urgent attachment cries for help

Amanda Jones

Introduction: the perinatal period and the origins of attachment

The etymological root of the word "perinatal" holds much meaning. In earlier times, "peri" denoted a "surround", and in today's context that pertains to the circular shape of a pregnant woman's womb that provides a stretching surrounding space for her baby to grow in. "Natal" meant, and means, a new, nascent life. Joined together, *peri-natal* takes us into a precious and precarious time span, namely the moment of conception to when a baby reaches toddlerhood. A pregnant woman's mind, both the aspect of mind of which she has some conscious awareness, and that aspect of mind that is dynamically alive yet outside of her awareness— her unconscious processes—together provide an ongoing emotional environment for her baby, and this continues in particularly important ways during her baby's early years of being alive, when attachment needs are most urgent and developmentally important. The same is so for the father, if he is able and allowed to contribute to this profound creative process. A new little person entering into the family offers the mother, father, grandparents, and siblings, opportunities to develop, struggle, change, mature, and grow, and come to know each other in new ways. For some mothers and fathers, the emotional demands and responsibilities can be too much, and in many different ways their caregiving capacities can be impaired. In the most risky situations, the parent's "surrounding emotional mind" can become ill. In the worst situations, the wider extended family is also disturbed, offering no emotional protection for the baby.

The perinatal period is precious because it offers hope, new life, and potential for growth for everyone involved, but it is also precarious because it is a time of enhanced vulnerability both physically and emotionally. It is a time of life that can become very risky for parents, perhaps especially for the mother, and for the baby. This chapter suggests that it is a risky time because a metaphorical plait of processes comes to the fore. First, the most powerful genetically driven emotional systems are necessarily in the foreground for baby and mother, father, and the wider family (Panksepp & Biven, 2012). These include not only primitive love and protectiveness and the urge to relate, but also the more difficult emotions of fear, rage, and panic. Second, unconscious processes have extraordinary power, and painful pre-existing vulnerabilities, hurts, and resentments can become freshly raw in the context of meeting a baby's needs and cries for help. Third, especially for the grown-ups most intimately involved in sacrificial parental care, primitive self-preservative defensive processes can be roused, and for some parents this can be very dangerous for their baby.

In the case I will describe a little about, baby Maisie's mother needed to use the defence of *denial* when exposed to Maisie's screams of pain: in mother Sarah's mind, Maisie was not in distress (evidence of denial), she was intentionally trying to reduce her mother to tears. This belief was intolerable and not thought about consciously until in therapy, but it understandably hardened mother Sarah and severed any possibility of an empathic response with Maisie. How come? What was going on in Sarah's mind? Maisie had been a planned-for and longed-for baby. In this brief description, we can see how Sarah's interpretation of her baby's distress vocalisation activated her own emotional response (linked to as-yet unthinkable childhood experiences) and then, quick as a flash, defensive processes were mobilised to try, desperately, to protect herself. These defensive processes would then influence her response and her behaviour when with Maisie's pain.

Given the complexity of what is going on in a mother's mind, a pre-verbal baby is helpless.

Parent–infant psychotherapy: the rationale for working with a parent and baby together

Before describing the therapeutic work and theoretical hypotheses in more detail, it makes sense to offer a rationale for a psychotherapy treatment that involves working with a parent and preverbal baby together, both during pregnancy and postnatally. The "patient" is their relationship and, by working with parent and baby together, their relationship is brought into the room. While this also happens in other situations, such as working with parents and older children in Child and Adolescent Mental Health Service settings, or in couple therapy, what is different about psychodynamic perinatal psychotherapy is the possibility to work at a very deep level with the adult parent's difficulties with the baby present. One aim is to facilitate more secure attachment responses from the baby. An hypothesis is that the baby lives with their parent's torment all day, every day, and there is a new experience for the baby of having another adult present and trying to help. What is different, disturbing, and difficult in parent–infant psychotherapy is the presence of the exquisite vulnerability of the new baby, the new life. In addition, there is the revived baby and small child in the mother.

During the first meeting with a suffering mother and baby, the parent–infant therapist's non-verbal communications will profoundly influence whether or not a trust can develop between the people present. If trust develops, the parent may begin to feel worrying, often frightening, sensations, and find at first unspoken words within their own mind whilst in the therapist's presence. Sometimes these silent words will tumble out and surprise the parent. Or the parent may censor the forming thoughts. Such forming thoughts will hopefully become vocalised in the therapeutic relationship, and bodily sensations and tension will be felt in the mother's body, the therapist's body, and the baby's body, as I describe in the clinical material to come.

For this experience of feeling safe enough to visit unsafe states of mind to happen, the therapist's non-verbal and vocalised communications need to convey a willingness to absorb and work with whatever is shared, no matter how disturbing. While absorbing disturbing emotional material, the therapist will be affected. The task is to try to understand what is occurring. For both parent and baby, confusing and unbearable emotional states will hopefully be experienced as, somehow, cared for and survived. These new memories then live alongside more traumatic experiences of, for example, a mother feeling humiliated and ashamed when vulnerable and distressed.

Parent–baby relationships: powerful emotions rouse primary defensive processes

This chapter will hone in on how the defensive processes roused in a mother, especially her defensive use of projection, can amplify her baby's difficulties in trying to regulate painful emotions of fear, panic, and rage. The neuroscientist Jaak Panksepp has a seemingly simple model to help us think about the genetically driven primary affective/ emotional systems that every baby and parent have to live with every day, moment to moment (Panksepp & Biven, 2012). These emotional systems can be exhausting to manage and often disrupt sleep, and include emotional states of fear, panic, and rage. Such emotions originate in deep areas of the brain and usually operate at a subcortical level. The emphasis here is that a parent with a baby has to cope with managing their own, often highly activated, primary emotional systems in the context of looking after their baby's. A mother's mind needs to be like a metaphorical absorbent muslin cloth: able to absorb the baby's distress; able to tolerate and work with her own distress that is roused due to feeling for her baby's distress; and she needs to be soft and strong and make effective decisions to help her baby become, in time, able to regulate his own emotional states.

It is vital a mother can feel empathy, and this entails being able to experience enough of her baby's distress to understand it while not experiencing the very same feeling herself. We could say that for all babies, there is a developmentally appropriate drive and evolutionary need to push difficult emotions, such as fear, panic, and rage, into the mother such that she *feels* the emotion. Why is this important? Peter Fonagy and other developmental researchers suggest that by *feeling* a concordant emotional state, the mother is conjoined to respond by trying to do some emotional work within her own body and mind in order to call up words to help her *think* about how to comfort, help, and protect her baby. This helps her baby to survive difficult experiences of surging emotions, such as fear, panic, and rage. An important emphasis is that, hopefully, the mother's feeling is *similar but not the same* as that expressed by her baby. This is why we can feel that a baby's distress gets into us. It literally does at an emotional biochemical neurological level. This is what is called empathy, and it can be very uncomfortable.

* * *

I will explore the particular problem that occurs when a mother's capacity to feel empathy for her baby is thwarted due to the over-activation of primary defensive processes that are unconsciously roused in the context of meeting her baby's dependency needs. Of importance when thinking about the problems that can erupt within a mother's mind is what "internal characters" come to life, so to speak, and what defences are mobilised to protect her from those internal characters. When I use the word "internal", I am suggesting that we carry around in ourselves, all the time, our experiences of having been looked after when we were little. If circumstances have been hard, there are many ways we can revise and work with these characters so that malignant experiences can become more benign. But if a mother has had a painful relationship with, for example, her own mother, and she has had no reparative experiences or therapeutic treatment, becoming a parent can pose a great risk. When trying to help such a parent, it is important to imagine and work out how her "internal characters" are operating, working away unconsciously, and rousing defensive responses. Mother Sarah had no way of knowing that very disturbing dynamics she experienced in her relationship with her mother would revive and haunt her relationship with baby Maisie.

* * *

I will describe the risks to the forming internal world of relationships and defensive processes for a baby like Maisie if a mother projects into her baby a particular constellation of feelings and beliefs about herself and her own internal mother (the mother she carries around in her mind based on her lived experiences of being cared for). These beliefs blur and confuse the mother's ability to interpret her baby's communications, and she is often not aware that ghostly experiences from her past are invading the present mother–baby relationship. She just feels depressed, agitated, and despairing, and behaves in defensively disturbing ways with her baby. The risks for a baby are considerable if such a situation is left without help. A baby like Maisie would be at risk of growing into a little girl who would not know how to ask for and use help when distressed.

A useful way of using the findings of attachment theory and research is to consider how a baby starts to develop self-preservative ways of trying to manage painful emotions *in the relationship* with their parent. The baby may well start to internalise and identify with its parents defensive strategies. This includes starting to internalise mother's intrusive projections as well as trying to keep mother out, so to speak. It is perhaps most useful to consider Peter Fonagy's suggestion that:

> attachment researchers often appear to reify attachment categories, considering them as theoretical entities rather than observed clusters of behavior. A problem arises if researchers cease to concern themselves with the mechanisms or psychic processes that may underlie such behavioral clusters. Beginning to think about these groupings in psychoanalytic terms, whether as habitual modes of defense or a manifestations of a representational system overinfluenced by paranoid-schizoid modes of functioning, might reduce the danger of reification of attachment categories. The psychoanalytic perspective might encourage us to think less categorically and more dimensionally about attachment security. The potential for both security and insecurity is likely to be present in all of us.
>
> (Fonagy, 2001, p. 187)

Mother Sarah and baby Maisie

Mother Sarah used the primary defensive processes of *projection* and *denial* to try to cope with her emotional collapse after baby Maisie's birth. Her emotional distress and defensive processes were suffusing, in an intrusive way, her baby's preverbal experience, influencing the growth of their non-verbal ways-of-being together such that I think baby Maisie was developing a schema-of-being-with-an-impervious-intrusive-mother. Impervious because Maisie's mother needed to try and keep out her baby's distress by becoming hardened and deaf to Maisie's cries, and intrusive because Sarah held some fixed ideas about Maisie that intruded into her baby. For example, her belief that Maisie deliberately wanted to reduce her mother to tears meant she did not want to pick up Maisie when she cried; she wanted to shut her in a room and walk away. The particular problem for five-month-old baby

Maisie was that her mother felt no sympathy or tenderness towards her. Maisie's mother's mind had become defensively hardened in response to the persecutory belief that her baby deliberately wanted to make her feel pain and shame: specifically, she believed her baby wanted to, and I quote, "reduce me to the point of tears". This belief foreclosed on any other way to hear her baby's screams. Sarah's wretched emotional state was conveyed in many non-verbal ways.

I use the example of mother Sarah to explore how she could not *absorb*, let alone feel about, and think about, her baby's distress and turmoil because she was too immersed in her own feelings and too in need of protecting herself from what she believed Maisie to feel. Therapeutic help would go some way to alleviating this.

* * *

At the start of treatment, baby Maisie was already highly avoidant of looking at her mother's face. She accurately perceived that her mother's expression would penetrate her in a disturbing way, so she showed signs of resisting this intrusion. When I use the word "avoidant" here, I mean that Maisie seemed to be trying to deny her mother existed. She used many ways not to look at her mother.

Sarah felt suicidal at the beginning of treatment. In the first session, Sarah described feeling an utter failure; she felt flung back into a quagmire of longstanding feelings of worthlessness, especially of failing to please her own mother, although this was not a conscious realisation when we first met.

We started treatment when Maisie was five months old. Yet Maisie was a planned-for and consciously wanted baby. How come her birth shattered her mother? Maisie stirred to life in her mother a particular set of *problematic unconscious projective processes*. It is not unusual when a mother has had a really difficult history herself, and no previous reparative experiences or therapeutic help, for the new baby to become confused with significant figures from her past, as well as disowned aspects of her own personality. The same is so for the father. The parent, so to speak, *transfers* their previous experiences in such a way that they become part of the current relationship.

Sarah was able to describe that being with Maisie, she felt as though in the presence of *an alien*, which we discovered was what she felt to be alien in her own mother. Also, Sarah had been deeply traumatised by the birth, requiring an emergency caesarean section. This made her feel physically abused and vulnerable, and Sarah felt her vulnerability to be disgusting, "an alien" to her. All of this was transferred/projected/ alive when in the presence of her crying baby.

This is why working with mother/father and baby together is so powerful. For if the baby, like Maisie, comes into the therapy room with her mother, these dynamics are brought in too: there is no hiding from the projections and the transference dynamics, no avoiding them. Maisie showed me her difficulties and, as her therapist, my emotional response to what I experienced in the room offered me critical information about the unconscious influences that might be disturbing the parent–infant relationship.

If a baby, like Maisie, experiences her mother as closed off to her communications, this may lead at times to the baby escalating and projecting her unbearable feelings more and more forcefully, with increased inconsolable screaming, as a desperate attempt to get through to her mother. The mother then feels intruded upon by a baby she experiences as impervious to her help or her milk. I witnessed this with Maisie and Sarah, and I saw how hardened Sarah became when Maisie cried. But beneath the armour of hardness, there was another Sarah, an inconsolable childlike Sarah who was terrified. It is understandable that she needed to distance herself from her true feelings.

A clinical moment that was painful but that helped

In the third session, I asked Sarah if she was dreaming. Sarah was managing to hold Maisie, and she described a vivid dream in which she was chased by a vampire. I made a comment about the dream: something about Sarah perhaps feeling chased by terrifying, life-threatening, vicious need. Sarah then linked the dream to feeling chased by Maisie's screaming needs the day she had the dream. She had shut her in her room, but Maisie's cries seemed to saturate the walls of the house. Then the theme of feeling chased led to thinking about her own mother. Sarah said she felt nervous, but her associations continued. She described how, when intoxicated and enraged, her mother would lock her in the house and chase her, before finally catching her and hitting her. The vampire then also possibly represented Sarah's unmet needs as a child, still chasing her, as well as her frightening mother, and her rage about of all of that, and more.

A little later, I made a comment about how I wondered whether the traumatic birth had felt like a similar physical assault. Sarah showed interest in this. I said, tentatively, how maybe this was because she could not bear to feel vulnerable and in physical pain and in the hands of a parent/doctor figure. This stirred more links with her mother, and she sobbed as she remembered feeling that her mother only stopped hitting when Sarah was reduced to tears.

Perhaps Maisie picked up on her mother's tension, perhaps an increased heart rate, stiffening muscles, I cannot be sure; all I know is Maisie became grizzly and then started crying in a way that was desperately difficult for Sarah. As Sarah had softened her defensive impenetrability with me, Maisie was, perhaps, in touch with her mother's pain, expressed through her body. Sarah tried to feed her, interpreting her grizzles as communications of hunger. But neither Maisie nor Sarah were nutritionally hungry: I think both were starving for something different to happen between them, but this could only happen in the presence of another caring person with a body and mind that could work with the feelings that erupted.

For a painful hour, I helped Sarah to stay with Maisie's screams. I resisted offering to take Maisie, offering instead gentle encouragement to Sarah to keep trying, reassuring her that I was there. Sarah wept whilst holding and rocking Maisie, saying how she needed to leave her. But she managed not to, and eventually Maisie settled and fell asleep, possibly defensively needing to shut down from the intensity of what had happened. What mattered was that Sarah did not abandon her whilst in the midst of her anguish.

Although Sarah could say that she had been so angry with me for, as she saw it, *making* her go through the experience of staying with Maisie's distress, by the end when I said that Maisie appreciated her staying with her, traces of a smile showed on Sarah's face as she wiped away her tears. She said if she had been at home, she would have put Maisie in another room. Sarah seemed to feel a sense of achievement that she had managed to stay with Maisie, and she kept hold of my words that Maisie was grateful for her sticking with it. Later that day, she successfully managed to do the same at home. At some level, she felt effective, successful, and this slightly shifted the pervasive sense of feeling a failure.

* * *

In the following weeks, I started to observe much more affection from Sarah towards Maisie. Maisie no longer felt like an alien to her mother, and the next phase of the work entailed helping Sarah understand and become more accepting of all that she felt was alien about herself, feelings that were inextricably linked to her deeply distressing relationship with her own alcohol-dependent mother. The work included coping with many difficult moments in the transference relationship, but Sarah showed considerable courage in persisting and working with some very, very painful emotional states.

While we were in the midst of this, Maisie was flourishing, the affection between Sarah and Maisie was palpable, and Maisie could start to feel herself in the presence of a mother who was not terrified by her distress. Maisie's cries could now be heard.

Conclusion

In this case, I have particularly highlighted how a mother's defensive need to be hard and impervious, plus the intrusion of the mother's hostile beliefs/projections, is extremely disturbing for a baby. I am grateful to a paper by Wilhelm Skogstad called "Impervious and intrusive: the impenetrable object in transference and countertransference" (2013), published in the *International Journal of Psychoanalysis*, for helping me to revisit the clinical material of Sarah and Maisie, with whom I worked several years ago. Hopefully, it has deepened my understanding about their tremendous difficulties being in close proximity with one another. Skogstad uses a rich clinical example to hypothesise how a baby might come to internalise a mother who has been experienced as *impervious* to the ordinary projections and other communications from her baby (especially the genetically driven distress call that is always full of the baby's primary emotions such as panic, fear, and rage). More difficult still, Skogstad describes how the mother is also experienced as *intrusive* in the sense that the mother projects into her baby certain disturbing beliefs and expectations. This can arise when the mother is disturbed, preoccupied, or traumatised, and easily drawn into a self-absorbed me-me-me state of mind in which her main goal is to defend herself from who she feels her baby to be. Mother Sarah's visceral response to Maisie's screams immediately triggered persecutory thoughts. She could not help but believe that her baby was deliberately trying to cause her distress, and her self-preservative response was to attack or flee or freeze to protect herself.

Skogstad introduces the idea that a baby like Maisie, if she had not been helped, would have possibly started to form an "impenetrable mother" within her mind and, in future, such an internal presence and influence might be extremely rejecting of any helpful attempt to get close to her or take care of her: in other words, the default position could become one of shutting down and pushing away potential help, thwarting the possibility of enjoying intimate emotional relationships.

* * *

Core to a mother like Sarah is what I can only describe as an abject feeling of, at some level, being filled with a black hole: an indescribable emptiness where "feeling loved" should be. She had felt unwanted, unloved, and that her mother wanted to hurt her. There is no worse place to be. When Maisie was born, in traumatic circumstances, Sarah believed that her baby was an alien who wanted to cause her harm and pain.

As mother Sarah used the therapy relationship to gain some insight into these confusions, her past experiences no longer haunted her day-to-day interactions with Maisie. Her mood improved, and Maisie started to be able to really use her mother's body and mind to help her with her big feelings, showing the progress she and her mother had made, and both became softer towards each other.

This is, necessarily, a simplified account of a complicated therapeutic process chosen to illustrate some theoretical points, especially the importance of helping the roused defensive processes in a mother when she is faced with ghosts from her past coming to life and suffusing her in terrifying ways when she has to meet the needs of her newborn baby.

Postscript

Although the case study distils relevant themes from several anonymized cases, recently the mother of one of the babies has been in contact. With her permission her updated account is important to share. At the beginning of treatment the mother was unable to bond with her baby but, with considerable courage, she worked on many of the issues described in the paper. Quite quickly into the parent–infant psychotherapy treatment she began to feel able to welcome and help her baby's attachment needs. In many ways their relationship flourished. However, during the subsequent years it became apparent that her baby grew into a child who had an underlying condition. She developed serious social and communication difficulties. Now, approaching adolescence, she has a diagnosis of autism/Asperger's syndrome (which her father has also been diagnosed with). Her mother described how, without addressing her own issues in the therapy, she would not have been able to adapt to the unique needs of her child. She described her evident commitment to ensuring her child's needs are recognised at school and she is able to provide the additional emotional understanding within the home. As she said, it is very hard work but her bond with her child helps her to manage. Parent–infant psychotherapy cannot prevent the emergence of an underlying condition but it can powerfully influence how a mother responds to such painful challenges.

References

Fonagy, P. (2001). *Attachment Theory and Psychoanalysis.* New York: Other Press.

Panksepp, J., & Biven, L. (2012). *The Archaeology of Mind: Neuroevolutionary Origins of Human Emotions.* New York: W. W. Norton.

Skogstad, W. (2013). Impervious and intrusive: the impenetrable object in transference and countertransference. *The International Journal of Psychoanalysis, 94:* 221–238.

CHAPTER THREE

The Adult Attachment Interview: information processing and the distinguishing features of preoccupied attachment

Or

What has attachment theory ever done for us?

Steve Farnfield

This chapter looks at information processing in the preoccupied Type C attachment strategies, focusing on the speech patterns identified by work on the Adult Attachment Interview (AAI). In attachment terms, "information processing" refers to ways in which the mind processes information about external threat and sexual opportunity. Most of this processing goes on at an unconscious somatic level. The theory section outlines Bowlby's concept of defensive exclusion (the exclusion of information which, if it were brought to consciousness, would cause us to suffer) and the array of Type C strategies described by Crittenden's Dynamic Maturational Model (DMM) of attachment. This is followed by sections on information processing and memory systems, together with a few examples. The final section looks at therapeutic implications.

Introduction to Type C

Type C strategies are referred to in the literature by a number of terms such as anxious ambivalent, preoccupied, coercive, and obsessive. The distinguishing features are ambivalence about close relationships (Do you really want me? How do I know that you love me? Are you secretly planning to leave me?), together with intense displays of attachment-seeking behaviour that can take the form of excessive anger or demands for rescue. Whereas in the world of Type A, attachment behaviour is terminated too soon, in Type C it is extended longer than necessary. Rather than comfort and security, which allows attachment behaviour to be turned down, the person in Type C feels safest (in strategy) when they are actually engaged in a struggle. (Throughout this chapter, people are referred to as being in Type C. This is to avoid seeing the person in terms of the strategy.) This can reach the point where a solution to a relationship problem is actually perceived as threatening because, without the problem, there is no struggle and the subject feels invisible.

A good way to think about coercive Type C behaviour in small children is the "terrible twos". This allegedly troublesome developmental period features in many northern European countries (the Norwegians have a statue, in Oslo, of a screaming toddler they call *Sinnataggen* or *Spitfire*), but is actually unknown in some other cultures and societies. This is of itself important. While the number of attachment strategies appears finite, they are distributed in different proportions according to culture. The British, who until recent demographic changes were a Type A culture (home of the "stiff upper lip"), find the behaviour of both toddlers and adolescents difficult to the point of deviant. On the other hand, Type C cultures (much of the Mediterranean basin comes to mind) are more comfortable with expressed emotion and appear to find children likeable.

In the terrible twos, Joel stamps his feet and when mother comes to help, he refuses any form of consolation, while his sister Joleen can scream and scream until she makes herself sick (the early stages of deliberate self-harm). What started as diffuse infant anxiety has now been organised strategically: protesting functions to maintain the attention of adults, who offer intermittent positive reinforcement of negative child behaviour, meaning they only attend to Joel for some of the time and then only when he is doing things they say they don't want him to do. This is confusing for Joel, particularly when his Mum shouts "don't do that" but then laughs. Joel works out that what she says is a poor guide to what she actually wants or will do, and so he ignores her verbal commands and focuses instead on her non-verbal clues, and on his own feelings and behaviour. With practice, Joel gets good at it. So does Joleen. She can use helplessness to the point where it becomes passive aggression. Now in first school, she can't tie her shoes, is frightened of loud noises, and sits close to the teacher without actually doing any work.

The infant Type C pattern was part of Ainsworth's original ABC typology using the Strange Situation Procedure (SSP) in which eleven- to fifteen-month-old babies are separated from their mothers for three minutes (Ainsworth, Blehar, Waters, & Wall, 1978). Of particular interest is the child's behaviour on reunion. In Type C, the amount of exploration or play in the SSP is limited compared to the other groups. Infants in Type C want to be close to their carers, get very upset when they leave, but rather than being pleased to see them on return, they either sit helplessly and cry or approach while showing signs of anger (pouting, drawing away when picked up, kicking, and so forth).

In Western samples, the proportion of infants assessed as being in Type C in the SSP is no more than six to seven per cent (Cassibba, Sette, Bakermans-Kranenburg, & Van IJzendoorn, 2013). The balance increases in the pre-school years and then falls off again (NICHD, 2001). The reason for this appears to be that Type C organisation requires a degree of cortical integration that infants lack. By the end of the second year, children are able to experiment with a coercive strategy (the terrible twos), but many of them reorganise into Type B when they learn that language is a better way of resolving difficulties and getting what they want, rather than escalating conflict.

Studies using the AAI with normative (i.e., relatively safe or non-clinical) adult populations show a surprisingly low number of people in Type C, around nine to eleven per cent (Cassibba et al., 2013).

The DMM Type C strategies

The DMM is developmental and maturational, which means attachment strategies can expand as we mature and as we experience changes in our environment (for full accounts of the model, see Crittenden & Landini, 2011; Farnfield & Holmes, 2014; Farnfield, Hautamäki, Nørbech, & Sahhar, 2010; Holmes & Farnfield, 2014). The full array of Type C strategies is given in Figure 1.

Crittenden's DMM Type C strategies			
Type C1–2	Threatening/ disarming	Develops in infancy/pre-school years	The odd-numbered C1/3/5/7 strategies are organised around anger.
Type C3–4	Aggressive/ feigned helpless	Pre-school years	
Type C5–6	Punitive/ obsessed with rescue	School years	The even-numbered C2/4/6/8 strategies are organised around the desire for comfort and fear of abandonment or attack.
Type C7–8	Menacing/ paranoid	Adulthood	

Figure 1. Crittenden's DMM type C strategies.

Type C1–2 develops in infancy and the pre-school years. Threatening behaviour signals to the parent "you know what I can do", while disarming behaviour (literally laying down your weapons) involves displaying a cute, adorable self to soften a covert lack of co-operation. Parents of these children are intermittently attentive and pay more attention to negative than co-operative child behaviour. Neither threats ("Do that again and I'll put you to bed") nor bribes ("Stop shouting and I'll give you a lolly") are acted on consistently, so the child learns to distrust parental commands (cognitive information about what will happen next) and instead uses her own feelings and behaviour to threaten or charm her carer into giving her what she wants. Another likely source of Type C1–2 is parental guilt, for example over-compensating for a busy work schedule by indulging their child during "quality time".

Type C is intensely interpersonal. By alternating threat (C1) with disarming (C2) behaviour, the child learns to regulate parental attention and anger. It's all about "focus on me".

The C1–2 pattern in children and adults carries no significant risk to psycho-social functioning (Crittenden & Landini, 2011) but is distributed in different proportions depending on culture (Van IJzendoorn & Sagi-Schwartz, 2008). Societies such as the UK, Germany, and the USA that value individualism over the group tend to have more people in Type A, while those such as Italy, Israel, and Japan, which value putting the wider family and the group before the self, produce more in Type C

(Crittenden & Claussen, 2000; Miyake et al., 1985; Oppenheim, Sagi, & Lamb, 1988; Takahishi, 1986; Van IJzendoorn & Kroonenberg, 1988).

Some children will remain in Type C1–2 all their lives; others will reorganise to another pattern; and in the pre-school years some may deepen the C strategy to C3–4. This is the easiest of the Type C patterns to determine because the behavioural signals are communications intended to be read by adults. If teacher doesn't "get it", do more of it until she does: anger in Type C3 and feigned helplessness in C4. While pre-schoolers in Type C4 do not get picked up for services (there is always an adult there to rescue them), Type C3 is the source of a multiplicity of referrals involving labels such as attention deficit hyperactivity disorder (ADHD), conduct disorders, or sometimes autistic spectrum disorders.

A feature of children in Type C3–4 is that, unlike Type C1–2, their behaviour is not confined to the home but is a more generalised way of organising the self in relationships. Anger in C3 is pervasive and seems to have no obvious cause. Feigned helplessness in C4 curtails the child's ability to explore and learn new things.

Parents of children in Type C3 are inconsistent and also deceive the child, for example by encouraging Joel to bounce up and down on the sofa then punishing him when he knocks over a lamp. Such children are frequently involved as pawns in parental arguments, so that the child is aware of being part of the problem but unclear as to why things happen as they do. Dad, for example, gets Joel to whoop as they play fight, knowing Mum will complain, and Dad can use this as an excuse to go to the pub. Other children in C3 are constantly criticised and sometimes humiliated by their attachment figures, harbouring a rage with everyone and everybody.

Children in the feigned helpless Type C4 pattern can be seen as reluctant caretakers. At least one of their parents punishes anger and exploration and needs the child to stay close to them. The outside world is presented as being full of unseen dangers involving, for example, paedophiles, child abductors, and bullies.

A point of interest is that SSP codings of chimpanzees brought up by humans produced a number in Type C4. When their human carers left them alone, the chimps lay on the floor, and on reunion bared their neck and belly waiting for their human attachment figure to pick them up. These animals were demonstrating a defence mechanism available to many species, but they were using it to excess. If they behaved in a similar way in the wild, they would have been killed. What do we learn from this? Feigned helplessness is a human neurosis! Parents of children in C4 reinforce desire for comfort and restrict their child's exploration, presumably because they need their child to need them (Jakubauskas, 2015).

Type C5–6 is developmentally possible in the school years. A feature of the environment of children in C5 is unpredictable danger from, for example, parental substance misuse, domestic violence, mental illness, or covert marital infidelity. When adults and older siblings exploit the child's efforts to obtain comfort and nurture, he organises around anger and dismisses his own vulnerability. Rather than the overt anger of C3, the C5 strategy is one of stealth and deception: *do not display your intentions until you know what the other person will do.* Anger is controlled and any perceived weakness in others is exploited.

In Type C6, the reverse is the case. Desire for comfort is intensified to an obsession with rescue while anger is hidden. The C6 strategy is self-protective in environments where overt displays of anger or resistance lead to trouble. Like those in C5, these children are enmeshed in family conflicts they only partially understand. Whereas people in C5 will risk the self to get revenge (murdering their partners for real or perceived infidelity), those in C6 will risk their own lives to elicit rescue. This leads to self-harming and other forms of high risk-taking behaviour.

In Type C7–8, the distortions of information processing (see below) are such that the role of the self in causing problems is denied and the role of others not just exaggerated but distorted. In this pattern, the self is either all-powerful (C7 menace, delusions of magic omnipotence) or utterly vulnerable, with paranoid ideas about the threat posed by others (C8). Whereas the perception of danger in C5–6 is focused on specific individuals or groups (racist ideology makes great use of the C5 mindset), in C7–8 everything is potentially dangerous. As children, adults in this pattern were often seduced into feeling safe then abused, so comfort itself is now deemed impossible.

Information processing—what does it mean?

Information processing refers to the ways in which the brain receives information about the body and uses it to survive. The information crucial to survival concerns food, shelter, sexual opportunity, and fight/flight from predators. Most of this processing goes on at an unconscious level. Humans have evolved higher cortical capacities that enable them to reflect on some aspects of information processing. This has certain benefits, in particular scientific, technological, and artistic exploration, together with the ability to co-operate with each other, what Fonagy and colleagues see as the evolutionary benefit of mentalizing (Fonagy, Lorenzini, Campbell, & Luyten, 2014). It also has disadvantages, in particular neuroses, PTSD, and—the reverse of socially co-operative mentalizing—genocide (Gray, 2002). Seen in this light, the overall benefits of high-functioning information processing appear dubious, but we are stuck with them.

The study of information processing is really the contribution that contemporary psychology and neuroscience is making to the old philosophical question of consciousness. All living things, whether plants, fish, fowl, or mammals, continually process information about their environment. Put another way, when information processing ceases, the organism is dead.

Consciousness is awareness that information processing is going on. But rather than cognitive activity (thinking), most decision-making is somatic and emotional. This is the basis of Damasio's critique of Descartes (Damasio, 1994): "Evidence that we are conscious is proven by the ability to think" (paraphrasing Descartes); "No, René. What you are really acting on is *feelings*, what your conscious mind calls emotions. The mind is an organ of the body not the other way round."

The major contribution by attachment studies to this debate is the Adult Attachment Interview (AAI), which looks at how people process information about threat, safety, and sexual opportunity (George, Kaplan, & Main, 1984). Of particular interest are transformations of information; instances where we omit or distort information in order to minimise suffering. This is what Bowlby termed defensive exclusion (Bowlby, 1980). Take, for example, the following exchange:

Simone: Do you remember how you felt when Mum died?
Simon: I went out into the garden. (Pause) Funny. I never realised just how strong the scent of hyacinths can be. (Pause) We'd better get back.

What can we learn from this fragment? Simon uses patterns of speech (discourse) suggesting a Type A form of defensive exclusion. The first thing Simon did was move to the garden. There, he pauses and recalls the strong olfactory sensation of the flowers. This stirs other memories, leading to the possibility of further integration ("funny"), but he dismisses them by remarking on their strangeness and cutting off any further reflection. The information about how he felt when he first heard his mother was dead is retained in the smell of the flowers. This enables him to keep the intensity of the experience without re-experiencing the emotions.

* * *

Building on developments in neuroscience, the DMM gives Bowlby's concept of an internal working model (IWM) an upgrade in terms of dispositional representations (DRs). Based on Damasio (1994, 2000), representations in the mind/body of danger to the self or to our children, or opportunity for sex, create a disposition to act. Whereas Bowlby's IWM suggests a somewhat static image, we actually have multiple images or representations of the same relationship or set of circumstances.

As an example, take a few minutes to think about your relationship with somebody close to you—your sexual partner perhaps. Think of times when you desired them or they desired you, and other times when you were angry or disappointed with them and they with you.

Who is this person? On reflection, they might seem to be defined as much by the relationship you have with them and your perception of them as any intrinsic characteristics they bear. When DRs fire off in the brain in the same direction, we can talk about integration—information is pointing in the same direction. But sometimes it doesn't. "I adore my lover; he excites me and wounds me. How I hate him!"

Integration in Type B secure attachment involves conscious awareness of discrepancies in DRs. But the more dangerous the environment, the less time there is to think (integrate), and so people in the higher DMM Type A+ and C+ subpatterns have to cut corners. In Type C, this corner-cutting involves, as we go down the model from C1 to C8:

- self as victim (found in all C patterns but increasing in intensity from C1 to 7–8);
- vagueness as to how things are connected;
- separating feelings of anger and desire for comfort;
- blaming others;
- deceiving others;
- deceiving the self in order to more successfully deceive others;
- distorting the role of self and threat posed by others.

Mentalizing

The degree to which the mind can accommodate discrepant information can be thought about in terms of mentalizing. Fonagy and colleagues developed the mentalizing concept from Bion's lovely metaphor of secure attachment—the container/contained—in which a crucial function of an attachment figure is to hold her baby not just with her arms but her mind. In this way, the baby learns how to think about herself and then about others. Top-drawer mentalizing means being known and understood by our parents so that we in turn can understand that other people have states of mind that may not chime with our own. It's the old untangling of my stuff from your stuff.

Fonagy and colleagues propose that: "mentalizing—attending to mental states in oneself and others—is *the most fundamental common factor* among all psychotherapeutic treatments" (Allen, Fonagy, & Bateman, 2008, p. xi, their italics). In attachment terms, rather than trying to make wholesale changes in self-protective strategies, there is a persuasive case for seeing the therapeutic task as facilitating an increase in the capacity for mentalizing.

Seen in this light, the differences between the DMM Type C subpatterns are degrees in distortions of mentalizing, or the ability to integrate competing dispositional representations. In Type C1–2, the level of danger is not particularly great and so the person does not have to come to a conclusion regarding competing DRs. This leads to the vague, involving nature of the discourse in AAIs rated C1–2 (see below). Away from attachment figures, children in C1–2 can function perfectly well to the point where they are hard to differentiate from securely attached peers. As we go down the model, the potential space, using Winnicott's term, for reflective integration becomes narrower and the playful gap between self and strategy ever more constricted (Winnicott, 1971).

In Type C3–4, the display of anger and/or vulnerability is more exaggerated than in Type C1–2, but access to the split-off parts of the self (vulnerability in C3 and anger in C4) is still possible under safe non-threatening conditions such as therapy. At C5–6, the split between anger and vulnerability is wider, and the use of deception (of self and others) makes integration much harder than in the lower Type C patterns. By C7–8, comfort is deemed impossible and overtures of reassurance and nurture, from a therapist or others, may be misconstrued as covert attempts to mislead the subject into believing he is safe in order to abuse him.

Memory systems

The DMM-Adult Attachment Interview (DMM-AAI) uses a system of discourse analysis (looking at patterns of speech) based on memory systems. These were identified from the literature by Bowlby (1980), developed by Main and Goldwyn in their prototype version of the AAI coding (Main & Goldwyn, 1984) and expanded by Crittenden (Crittenden & Landini, 2011, see Figure 2) using work by Damasio (1994, 2000) and Schacter and Tulving (1994). While the use of the term "memory systems" is not wholly congruent with the current neuroscience, it serves as a useful description of different forms of information processing.

* * *

The model is based on the three accepted dimensions of mental functioning: cognition, affect, and motivation. In the DMM, cognition simply refers to temporal order or what appears to cause what. Using AAI discourse, an example is "When Father was drunk, I knew I had to lock my door."

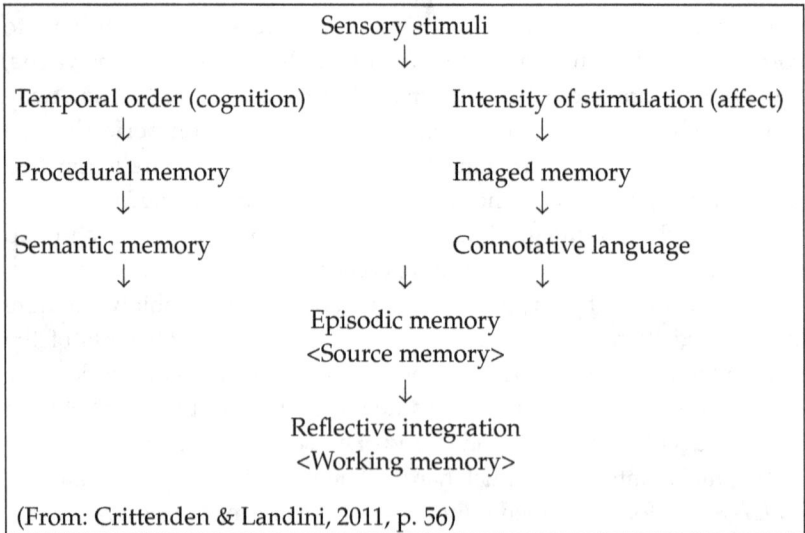

Sensory stimuli
↓

Temporal order (cognition)   Intensity of stimulation (affect)
            ↓   ↓
Procedural memory   Imaged memory
            ↓   ↓
Semantic memory   Connotative language
            ↓   ↓   ↓

Episodic memory
<Source memory>
↓

Reflective integration
<Working memory>

(From: Crittenden & Landini, 2011, p. 56)

Figure 2. Transformations of information: the organisation of information and memory systems.

Affect refers to physiological arousal that may be very low, as in depression, and passes through tiredness, boredom, to more alert states and then up through anger, sexual desire, pain, and mania. In attachment studies, motivation involves self-protection, sex and reproduction, and protection of our children.

Starting with cognition, procedural memory is unconscious (implicit) behaviour learned through experiences with attachment figures when we are infants. This is what the Ainsworth SSP assesses: What has the baby learned to expect from mother when he is distressed? What will he do when Mum comes back into the room? In therapeutic terms, these unconscious expectations can be thought about as the transference, and the client's perception of the therapist's responses to distress are likely to be influenced by such experiences.

Semantic memory develops in the second and third years through language and involves cognitive statements regarding parental expectations of the child's behaviour. "Good girl, you tidied away your toys"; the subtext is that Mummy approves of girls who put away their toys.

On the affect side of Figure 2, imaged memory refers to all of the five senses, with sensations of touch, taste, and smell carrying particular potency. All memories are in fact imaged, written on the body, but in terms of the AAI, imaged statements such as "I loved the smell of my granny" or "The bed was freezing" are useful indicators as to the way a particular person organises around feelings and, in the case of early memories, important things that might have gone on before language.

Connotative language is Crittenden's sole contribution to this model of memory systems and refers to the way we use language to control the affective states of the self and other people. Take the client who is boring, who drones on, leaving the therapist feeling drowsy and unable to concentrate. The client seems to be signalling "there is nothing interesting about me, stay away". This is an example of connotative language in Type A. In Type C, language is used to pump up the self for action and to involve the therapist. "My mother? Huh, she's been dead ten years but the bitch still lives in my mind like a cancer. She's a crab. You know the type? Claws in my head." The client makes pincer movements in the air, bringing mother crab into the room (an *animated image* in AAI terms).

* * *

At the age of three to four years, integration of cognitive and affective information enables what we usually think of when we talk about memory, a specific time when something happened. This is episodic memory, for example: "One night, Dad was drunk and I had to lock my bedroom door. Mum was out and I could hear him downstairs talking to himself about me, so I called my sister but ..." And so we get a complete story or episode.

Episodic memory in children under six years is co-constructed with adults, after which children can develop accounts of what happened independently. Thus an important aspect of episodic memory is knowing how we know about something. Comments such as: "Do I remember it, or is it because my uncle has a photograph of us all? I'm not sure" are common. The speaker is aware that he cannot be certain of the source of information.

Problems occur for people who are confused and omit the source of information by attributing too much of what happened to the self. For example: "I remember vividly my mother breastfeeding me when I was no more than four months old. The radio was on." This is not possible. In the DMM-AAI, it is referred to as "disorientation". DRs of other people and the self at different ages are all lumped together, giving the subject huge difficulties in organising either an A or C strategy to the extent that they flip flop from cognitive to affective information without ever finding a perspective that works. Clients in this vein are both confused and confusing, and likely to confuse the thinking of the therapist.

The only fully explicit (conscious) memory system is working or integrative memory. Le Doux (2002) calls this a "work space"—a place where we bring information to consciousness in order to work on our DRs. This requires both time and safety, and is what happens in therapy.

Unresolved trauma and loss modifiers

An attachment strategy is just that—strategic. It functions to protect the self. Adults often come to therapy because a strategy that was functional in childhood no longer works in adulthood. This from a well-informed interviewee: "My Type C4—hell, I read all the goddam textbooks—was fine when I was at home with my sick mother, but now I am married it's driving my partner away. I'm too clingy. I'm scared of being left alone. I tell him 'you masturbate, it's a betrayal'. I make him come home every lunch-time and make love to me. Now he wants me to see a shrink. Is that fair?"

Strategies may also suffer—sometimes only momentary—disruption from unresolved trauma or loss. Like all strategies, the C1–8 patterns enable the subject to organise around difficult experiences, but not all of them. As a rule of thumb, we can say that anyone in C5 and above is also likely to be traumatised or suffering unresolved loss. Unresolved losses and traumas are not pervasive but derail a functioning strategy when DRs are activated in a particular context.

In the DMM-AAI, lack of resolution takes a variety of forms including: preoccupied ("it's not over"), dismissing ("it meant nothing"), vicarious (taking on an attachment figure's trauma), anticipated loss or trauma (with no evidence to support it), imagined or hinted (to mislead the therapist into thinking something bad happened), and delusional (various forms, including delusional revenge on the perpetrator).

More serious, because they are a pervasive form of disruption to strategies, are DMM modifiers. These include: disorientation (see the example above), depression, expressed somatic symptoms (bad things that cannot be talked about are expressed through bodily symptoms such as tics, coughing, yawning, scratching, and so on), and reorganisation to a more secure strategy or more integrated form of information processing (see Crittenden & Landini, 2011). In serious examples, modifiers may actually cripple the functioning of a strategy over long periods.

What does the AAI assess?

The originators of the AAI protocol commented that the interview was designed to surprise the unconscious (George et al., 1984). Whereas self-report questionnaires (e.g., Bartholomew & Horowitz, 1991) tap into conscious semantic memory, the AAI flushes out attempts to exclude information from the self and others. In this regard, it is rather like following a Pinter play: the real story is not in the surface speech but the pauses, silences, and things people do not say, or say in ways designed to disguise their true meaning.

Specifically, the interview assesses the speaker's state of mind with regard to his or her childhood attachment relationships. What happened (the content) is less important than the coherence of the narrative. From a therapeutic perspective, it is an exercise in active listening in which the therapist asks herself: "Is my client speaking as the child they were when these things happened, or are they able to comment on them from the vantage of maturity?"

A DMM-AAI analysis yields:

- a self-protective strategy in Type A, B, or C;
- modifiers;
- unresolved loss or trauma;
- an account of how this particular speaker processes information according to different memory systems.

For the therapist, it is likely the last point that is the most useful.

The AAI is audio-taped and then transcribed so that what starts as a conversation ends as a script. The transcription includes all the stutters, pauses, and dysfluencies (the way we actually speak) so that the coder can detect possible points of defensive exclusion.

Figure 3 lists an abbreviated account of the types of questions in the AAI together with the memory system(s) they probe.

* * *

---

1. Tell me about your early childhood, where you lived, what your parents did for a living, that kind of thing (integrative memory).
2. What's the first thing you can remember (imaged)?
3. Give me five adjectives to describe the relationship you had with your mother (then father) (semantic).
4. You described the relationship with your mother as V, W, X, Y, and Z. Starting with V, give me a time when the relationship was V (episodic).
5. Questions about normative childhood dangers such as illness and brief separations (episodic).
6. Questions about potential traumatic experiences including abuse (episodic).
7. Questions about losses in childhood and adulthood (episodic).
8. Integrative questions such as "Why do you think your parents treated you in the way that they did?"

Figure 3. Examples of questions used in the AAI.

Procedural memory
Discourse Involved/preoccupied with others (C1–4) Dismissing others' feelings/perspective (C5–8) *Arousal* Disarming, e.g. laughing at negative remarks Intense negative affect Enjoying others' hurt or humiliation *Relationship with the therapist* Involving Collusion Submission Seduction Spooky
Imaged memory
Intense Animated—bringing the image into the room Delusional power or threat
Connotative language
Evocative, arousing, poetic
Semantic memory
Passive semantic thought—coming to no conclusion when a semantic statement is required. "I left him because well … you know." Reductionist blaming thought—reducing a person to a problem in order to attack them: "All the police are bastards." "She never had a good word to say for me." (C3–4) Person-defined negative—negative descriptions that have a special/personal meaning to the speaker
Episodic memory
Blurred accounts in which several episodes are elided. Fragmented episodes—the speaker distorts how it happened and/or omits their part in the problem. Selective with the vérité (C3–6) Triangulated blame—involving one parent/person to attack or blame the other (C5–6)

Figure 4. (Continued).

Integration
Lack of integration
Pseudo-integration sometimes borrowed from previous therapies.
Rationalisation, self-justification
Skilful misleading—allowing the therapist to come to the wrong conclusion about the self.

Figure 4. Some examples of Type C discourse markers.

Examples

This section gives three examples that follow a theme common to Type C: dismissing other people's perspective, from pre-school through adolescence to adulthood. As with the DMM-AAI, these transcripts include the precise words, pauses, and dysfluencies of the interviewer and interviewees.

The first example comes from Griff, aged four. He is doing a narrative story stems exercise in which the interviewer, with the help of a few simple props, tells him the beginning of a story and then asks him to "tell me and show me what happens next".

Interviewer: Okay so Chair (the name chosen by Griff for his doll protagonist) is having tea with his family and he reaches out and Oh dear he's knocked over his juice. Tell me …

Griff: (Interrupts. Snatches the doll) He goes wee (laughing) and then his gran comes and then the baby his gran says you spilt your juice and the baby goes wee (shows the baby kicking Gran) but Dad is Dad is hanging like the baby pushes Dad and he's wee (shows Dad fall slowly from the roof of the doll's house) and then …

This is a good example of Type C3 cartoon violence from a four-year-old. Griff mocks the task (he chose the name Chair for the doll), uses run-on speech, and escalates problems. It's like watching a cartoon in which people do violent things to each other but nobody gets hurt. Powerful babies figure frequently in these stories, wreaking all kinds of vengeance on parents and siblings. Investigation into this pattern strongly indicates children like Griff are not traumatised, they have not been abused, but they are furious with parents who are inconsistent (see Farnfield, 2015). Rather than trying to control their parents and other people, what these children actually want is a greater sense that their parents have them in mind and are in control of them.

* * *

The second extract comes from a child attachment interview (Can you tell me? Farnfield, 2015) with Wesley, aged sixteen, who was living in a children's home.

> Interviewer: Were you happy at home?
> Wesley: No, not really, well, no not really, not at all, huh (slight dismissive laughter)
> Interviewer: Can you tell me why?
> Wesley: Er. I was getting beatings every time I walked in the house, so I go to school get beaten up at school as well, so that's pretty smart.
> Interviewer: You were beaten up at school (yeah) and then sounds to me like you got bashed at home too?
> Wesley: Yeah (by ?) that's why I'm in here anyway.
> Interviewer: The children's home? (yeah) Is this a happy place for you or not a happy place?
> Wesley: It's alright. I used to get picked on and then one day I had enough and beat someone up badly (slight laugh).
> Interviewer: You beat someone up?
> Wesley: No, I got beat, I kept getting beaten up every day and I had enough of it one day, grabbed hold of their head and put it on the floor and picked up a fire extinguisher and dropped it on their head (laugh).
> Interviewer: What did it do to them?
> Wesley: Oh they just fell unconscious. They kept beating me up and (yeah, yeah, I'm not er) just had enough, turned round ... lost my rag.
> Interviewer: Right.
> Wesley: Those bloody fire extinguishers weigh a ton (laughs).

This extract is coded Type C5. What stands out is how Wesley presents himself as a victim in order to justify dropping the fire extinguisher on the other boy's head, together with his disregard for the serious injury this would have caused. Like the cartoon violence in Griff's stories, there is some doubt as to whether it happened like this—is Wesley exaggerating his own power and minimising his own and other's vulnerability?

* * *

The third member of this trio is Tony, aged forty-five.

Tony: Yeah, I mean the er I can remember now when they used always to have big Christmases and all that and all the relations round and all this sort of thing they was always saying he's a bad boy that one (laughs).

Interviewer: (laughs) How old were you then, Tony?

Tony: About ten (both laugh).

Interviewer: They used to say that?

Tony: Yeah, because half the time they used to think that I was spoilt, you know putting it down to being spoilt, it wasn't that, I was just a hooligan.

Interviewer: Did you feel, as a child, did you feel different in some way?

Tony: No, no. You know, I used to get in trouble with the police and that. I'm the only one in our family that's ever been in trouble with the police. (uh—pause) None of my brothers or anything. They was never in trouble or anything. I can remember breaking my brother's leg. (Go on) cause my Mum was out, and er, I've come home, I was about sixteen then, sixteen or seventeen, and my Mum was out.

Interviewer: Who, he was how old?

Tony: Well, he would have been then, I was sixteen, he would have been twenty (yes right) and I've come home from work and we've started having argument. I can't remember exactly, we started fighting upstairs or something, so I've hit him on top of the stairs and he's fell down the stairs, he lay on top of the stairs and I've gone and jumped on his leg and broke his leg. There was big hoo-ha over that like, you know.

Interviewer: What happened?

Tony: He just had his leg set and there was big you know what went on and all this sort of thing, you know.

* * *

Note here the collusion between Tony and the interviewer, and Tony's pride in his delinquency (C5). The account of breaking his brother's leg has the cinematic quality of cartoon violence but the detail is ghoulish, suggesting Type C7–8. The interviewer commented, "The light was fading and the room was getting dark. Tony enjoyed having me as an audience, and after the tape recorder was turned off told me a story about how he nearly killed a man who upset his dog. I was glad to get out of the house."

Family systems

Attachment theory is relatively weak in its understanding of the contribution family and wider systems make to the formation of individual strategies. We all grow up in families, and from a systemic perspective no one part of a system functions without influencing other members. Of the A, B, and C strategies, Type C is most completely understood when looked at from the perspective of the family system. The childhoods of people in Type C feature enmeshed relationships where the boundaries between self and other are frequently blurred or distorted. As they grow up, the triangulated nature of relationships (the inability to refer to one person without drawing in another) continues into work, love, and therapeutic relationships. People in C are never alone. Even when there are just the two of us (you–me, Mum–Dad, therapist–client, and so on), the voices from other struggles permeate the conversation. This is an extract from an AAI with Judy, aged twenty-eight.

Interviewer: OK, so if you had to give me five words or phrases to describe the relationship with your Dad when you were young, what words would you use for him?

Judy: ... He was more proud.

Interviewer: Proud?

Judy: He was yeah, proud .... I don't remember being cuddled or anything.

Interviewer: By your dad?

Judy: No, I don't remember, I don't remember being cuddled but always being ... with him.... um....

Interviewer: OK, and how would you describe the relationship between the two of you when you were young?

Judy: I'd say it must have been good....

Interviewer: OK, anything else?

Judy: erm .... More loving.

Interviewer: Than your mum?

Judy: Yeah (laughs).

Later:

Interviewer: Do you think your childhood affected say, who you chose to be with, how do you think that affected you?

Judy: Well, my first boyfriend I had when I left home .... I'm pretty sure ... I don't ... I was probably a bit naïve and that then, he was into drugs I think but I didn't ... I wasn't aware of the drugs, I'd never seen them, but that was quite violent and scary and physical.

Interviewer: And you were, what, fifteen then?

Judy: Yeah.

Interviewer: And did you stay in that relationship or get out of it?

Judy: Erm .... I can't remember whether ... I ... we moved ... I stayed in his flat that him and his ex-girlfriend used to have and when I was and when I was there she used to do ... she used to turn up and cause trouble and then he left and I can't remember where he left because he left me in the flat and I used to go to work, come home and be on my own in that flat ... and then erm she turned up one day trying to break in and I just remember it being a whole scary ... screaming about her trying to get in and when I'd go to work she'd chop up all my stuff and I'd come back and it was just horrible.

Judy is asked about her relationship with her Dad and starts by comparing him more favourably with her mother, but the person who completes the negative comparison is the interviewer! Note Judy's laugh as the interviewer obliges by finishing the attack. The second part involves love relationships, but Judy soon involves her boyfriend's ex-partner and a dispute in which Judy's part appears to be that of victim. Judy was admitted to an inpatient unit following bouts of self-harming and a suicide attempt. Her interview was coded Type C6 with family triangulation.

Mental health problems typical in Type C

In terms of psychiatric diagnoses, Type C strategies are evident in personality disorders, conduct disorders, and attention deficit hyperactivity disorder (ADHD). They also feature in people who have a history of risk-taking (including self-harm) and antisocial behaviour. In a study of women with eating disorders, the most common pattern was unresolved imagined trauma C5–6 with strong evidence of family triangulation, sometimes paired with a Type A strategy (Ringer & Crittenden, 2007). The latter example is coded A/C, meaning the subject alternates A and C strategies, or AC when the two strategies are blended (false affect with false cognition), which is a feature of psychopathy.

The hypothesis regarding eating disorders is that, as children, these clients were confused regarding parental behaviour which was, in reality, tied to family secrets (hidden marital conflict or parental trauma) they could not know about. Refusing to eat was used as a weapon in the perpetual struggle with parents that they could not win because they did not understand who or what the struggle was about or how it related to the self.

Therapeutic implications

The AAI offers the therapist an assessment tool that is finely calibrated for the experience of each particular client. This enables the therapist to formulate treatment plans using the engine of the AAI—information processing. In particular, we can gain an understanding of:

- memory systems: bias towards cognition or affect?
- information processing: what information is transformed or distorted?
- how is it transformed?
- how did this transformation enable the client to feel safer as a child?
- how does it function now?
- relationship with the therapist
- level of physiological arousal
- level of integration/mentalizing.

Modifiers (depression, disorientation, expressed somatic symptoms) are likely to need urgent attention, as will unresolved trauma and loss if it impinges on current psycho-social functioning. But attachment strategies may be left alone in favour of working with the client to expand on current strategies to include new, previously excluded information (mentalizing). For example, a client in Type C5 may be encouraged to experience his fear of displaying vulnerability through scaffolding the therapy. This might include episodic information concerning times when he was bullied as a child with cognitive appraisal of the effects of his anger on his relationship with his wife. The therapist should also consider in what way the proposed intervention might be dangerous for the client. Focusing, for example, on bodily sensations with a client who is engaged in high-risk encounters with older men (Type C6) might actually render her more vulnerable, or dwelling on the perceived bad qualities of his parents may actually reinforce a client's belief that he is justified in his plans to rob them.

From case experience, whereas clients in Type A usually know what their problem is but have no solution, those in Type C are acutely aware of being unhappy but either have no idea or erroneous ideas regarding the cause. Hence they may blunder from one therapist or one type of treatment to another in the hope of finding a solution. Where a number of professionals are involved with the same client or family, the triangulation which is a prominent feature of the C strategy can lead to splits, and sometimes heated disagreements, in the professional network. Another problem is collusion—the therapist is invited to *join my gang or become my enemy*.

Clients in Type C distort information so that the shadow of the expressed emotion is not always visible. At its simplest, this is the anger in passive aggression and the vulnerability in the angry patterns. Because the underlying fear in Type C is not being held in mind, clients may actually avoid implementing solutions to their problems, even when paying for the treatment, for fear of becoming invisible and being dumped by their therapist.

In the high C5–8 patterns, holding contradictory feelings about the same event or person is nigh impossible so that splitting becomes a feature of the relationship. Klein's ideas on paranoid-schizoid mechanisms neatly fit the C5–8 countertransference, whereby the therapist experiences feelings of panic, fear, rage, or disgust which their client can no longer tolerate. The therapist may then feel punitive or frightened of the client, thereby reinforcing the client's own feelings of paranoia. All of which indicates that a high degree of therapeutic skill is necessary for any progress to be made.

Conclusion

Q: What has attachment theory ever done for us?
A: Given us the concept of information processing.

Learning to code AAIs is an expensive and time-consuming business, but some familiarity with the method of discourse analysis and the DMM patterns of attachment may enrich professional practice and save a lot of professional time.

References

Ainsworth, M. D. S., Blehar, M., Waters, E., & Wall, S. (1978). *Patterns of Attachment*. Hillsdale, NJ: Erlbaum.

Allen, J. G., Fonagy, P., & Bateman, J. G. (2008). *Mentalizing in Clinical Practice*. Washington, DC: American Psychiatric Publishing.

Bartholomew, K., & Horowitz, L. M. (1991). Attachment styles among young adults: a test of a four-category model. *Journal of Personality and Social Psychology, 61*: 226–244.

Bowlby, J. (1980). *Loss, Sadness and Depression*, Volume 3: *Attachment and Loss*. New York: Basic Books.

Cassibba, R., Sette, G., Bakermans-Kranenburg, M. J., & Van IJzendoorn, M. H. (2013). Attachment the Italian way: in search of specific patterns of infant and adult attachments in Italian typical and atypical samples. *European Psychologist, 18*(1): 47–58.

Crittenden, P. M., & Claussen, A. (Eds.) (2000). *The Organization of Attachment Relationships: Maturation, Culture and Context*. New York: Cambridge University Press.

Crittenden, P. M., & Landini, A. (2011). *The Adult Attachment Interview: Assessing Psychological and Interpersonal Strategies*. New York: W. W. Norton.

Damasio, A. R. (1994). *Descartes' Error: Emotion, Reason and the Human Brain*. New York: Putnam.

Damasio, A. R. (2000). *The Feeling of What Happens: Body and Emotion in the Making of Consciousness*. London: Vintage.

Farnfield, S. (2014). Assessing attachment in the school years: the application of the dynamic maturational model of attachment to the coding of a child attachment interview with community and looked after children. *Clinical Child Psychology and Psychiatry, 19*(4): 516–534.

Farnfield, S. (2015). The child attachment and play assessment (CAPA): validation of a new approach to coding narrative stems with children aged 3 to 11 years. *International Journal of Play Therapy*. Online First Publication, 8 June 2015. http://dx.doi.org/10.1037/a0038726

Farnfield, S., & Holmes, P. (Eds.) (2014). *The Routledge Handbook of Attachment: Assessment*. London: Routledge.

Farnfield, S., Hautamäki, A., Nørbech, P., & Sahhar, N. (2010). DMM assessments of attachment and adaptation: procedures, validity and utility. *Clinical Child Psychology and Psychiatry, 15*(3): 313–328.

Fonagy, P., Lorenzini, N., Campbell, C., & Luyten, P. (2014). Why are we interested in attachments? In: P. Holmes & S. Farnfield (Eds.), *The Routledge Handbook of Attachment: Theory* (pp. 31–48). London: Routledge.

George, C., Kaplan, N., & Main, M. (1984, 1996). *Adult Attachment Interview*, unpublished, University of California at Berkeley.

Gray, J. (2002). *Straw Dogs: Thoughts on Humans and Other Animals*. London: Granta.

Holmes, P., & Farnfield, S. (Eds.) (2014). *The Routledge Handbook of Attachment: Theory*. London: Routledge.

Jakubauskas, R. (2015). Using the Dynamic Maturational Model of attachment to categorise attachment strategies in laboratory-reared one-year-old chimpanzees. Unpublished Masters thesis, University of Roehampton.

Le Doux, J. (2002). *Synaptic Self: How Our Brains Become Who We Are*. London: Macmillan.

Main, M., & Goldwyn, R. (1984.) *Adult Attachment Scoring and Classification System*, unpublished, University of California at Berkeley.

Miyake, K., Chen, S., & Campos, J. J. (1985). Infant temperament, mother's mode of interaction, and attachment in Japan: an interim report. In: I. Bretherton & E. Waters (Eds.), *Monographs of the Society for Research in Child Development, 50*: 276–297.

NICHD Early Child Care Research Network, Public Information and Communication Branch (2001). Child-care and family predictors of preschool attachment and stability from infancy. *Developmental Psychology, 37*(6): 847–862.

Oppenheim, D., Sagi, A., & Lamb, M. E. (1988). Infant–adult attachments on the kibbutz and their relation to socioemotional development 4 years later. *Developmental Psychology, 24*(3): 427–433.

Ringer, F., & Crittenden, P. M. (2007). Eating disorders and attachment: the effects of hidden processes on eating disorders. *European Eating Disorders Review, 15*: 119–130.

Schacter, D. L., & Tulving, E. (1994). What are the memory systems of 1994? In: D. L. Schacter & E. Tulving (Eds.), *Memory Systems* (pp. 1–38). Cambridge, MA: Bradford.

Takahashi, K. (1986). Examining the Strange Situation Procedure with Japanese mothers and twelve-month-old infants. *Developmental Psychology, 27*(2): 265–270.

Van IJzendoorn, M. H., & Kroonenberg, P. M. (1988). Cross-cultural patterns of attachment: a meta-analysis of the Strange Situation. *Child Development, 59*: 147–156.

Van IJzendoorn, M. H., & Sagi-Schwartz, A. (2008). Cross-cultural patterns of attachment: universal and contextual dimensions. In: J. Cassidy & P. R. Shaver (Eds.), *Handbook of Attachment: Theory, Research, and Clinical Applications* (2nd edn.) (pp. 880–905). New York: Guilford.

Winnicott, D. W. (1971). *Playing and Reality*. London: Tavistock.

CHAPTER FOUR

Don't ever threaten to leave me—and if I threaten, you'd better not believe it

Anne Power

The client who came back

I imagine that the reason most of us have gathered here under this theme is because we often find the work with this client group very challenging, and we would like to do better for them. I have had quite a slow learning curve with preoccupied patients, and I would like to start by sharing a case where I struggled with my countertransference, and regrettably acted on it. All the clinical work that I will mention has either been disguised or permission was given for its use.

When I chose this title, I had in mind Bowlby's (1973) observation that a parent's threats to leave a child can cause significant harm. People with a preoccupied strategy may or may not have received outright threats of abandonment, but almost certainly they have experienced an inconsistency in parental attention—whether these absences arose from depression, addiction, distracting anxiety, or any other kind of distress in the caregivers.

We see this dynamic in adult couple relationships where preoccupied people will use walking out as a way to regulate themselves in relationships, but they do this on the assumption that they can return when they feel ready. We often hear about couples where one person storms off now and again, often underestimating the distress experi-enced by the partner and family being walked out on. The departure may be only for a few hours, and the person who leaves does so with the firm assumption that they will return when they are ready. In some couples, the crisis point comes when the partner who has always stayed puts out signals that they have had enough and they want to call it a day with the relationship. The preoccupied person, who has been using the departures as a way to regulate the relationship, is likely to become very angry at this point, because in their mind they were never leaving, and their partner should have known that.

In this first anecdote, I will share a case where this "threat" to leave was taken too concretely by me. This case also illustrates how the therapist can be drawn into an enactment, which in this case played out the client's expectation of being rejected.

A new client, Anthony, had been coming to see me for a few weeks and the transference and countertransference felt uncomfortable. Although the first couple of sessions had seemed to go well, there was then a steep fall-ing off in collaboration and a sense of disappointment in both the client and me. This early rapport can happen with preoccupied clients, as their desire for help can initially create an immediate fit with the therapist's need to be useful. Things soon changed, and from the third week Anthony had doubts as to whether he wanted to continue, while I felt blamed by his expecta-tion that I should be achieving more. When we came to the sixth week, the point at which I aim to decide with clients whether we will now commit to open-ended work, Anthony told me he did not want to continue. While I went through the motions of exploring this, I think really I was relieved at his decision. I said goodbye feeling both rejection and relief, and after a short break opened the door to my next client, whom I will call client B. A few weeks prior to this, client B had asked me if I had an earlier appoint-ment free, as a change in her work hours had made her current time quite difficult. I had explained that I didn't have an earlier space but would let her know if anything came up. As I sat down to work with client B, I opened by mentioning that I could now offer her the change she had been hoping for; she was very pleased and we had the session. When I finished the session, I saw a call on my answerphone and found a message from Anthony: he had realised he had been precipitate and said he would like to come back next week and think about this with me. When I rang him, I had to say that

I could no longer do that exact time, I could do later that day, and I was able to offer a time on another day. Not surprisingly, he was angry and hurt and declined my offer, reasonably articulating that he thought I could have waited a bit longer before giving away his time.

I think we can see a number of dynamics operating here. There is a concrete practical issue: there is an enactment of rejection, and perhaps in addition there is an oedipal displacement. Client B had been wanting the earlier slot for a good reason, but my haste in giving it away had at least a whiff of revenge against Anthony. When an hour later, listening to my messages, I discovered that Anthony had been more mature than me, that he had been able to think again about our exchange and was willing to risk re-approaching me, I felt somewhat humbled and was very sorry that his willingness to try again had met an obstruction on my part. Having found the courage to return, he had discovered that he had already been dispensed with and his place filled by another; no wonder he felt the need to reject my offer of a new time.

The preoccupied strategy

As we have been reflecting in this book, people with preoccupied strategies live in fear of losing their significant other, they over-attend to their negative feelings of fear and anger, and sometimes express these in an exaggerated way. This amplification of feelings can increase anxiety in the person *themselves* as well as alienating those around them. This chronic attachment insecurity is sustained by a very bleak set of internal working models: a model of self as needing care but not deserving it; a model of other as able to give care but not willing to do so. Mikulincer and Shaver summarise the combination thus: "energetic attempts to attain greater proximity, support and love combined with a lack of confidence that it will be provided" (Mikulincer & Shaver, 2010, p. 272). They also point to the relentless quality of the experience:

> Although anxiously attached people have a history of frustrating interactions with attachment figures, they still believe that if they intensify their proximity-seeking efforts, they may force relationship partners to pay attention and provide adequate support.
>
> (Mikulincer & Shaver, 2010, p. 273)

Johnson and Whiffen point out how harmfully self-perpetuating this defence is, how effectively it impedes learning in these patients: "It is difficult to revise what one cannot access, coherently articulate and evaluate" (Johnson & Whiffen, 1999, p. 374).

Attachment research has proposed various ways of subcategorising the insecure patterns. Crittenden, Dallos, Landini, and Kozlowska (2014) use two terms that highlight intentionality: they describe coercive aggression and coercive feigned helplessness. The aggressive strategy is provocative, and so the child using this defence needs also to have a strategy for disarming parental anger; she achieves this through a switch to an exaggerated desire for comfort. Occasionally, we work with a client who presents in the room with precisely this oscillation between defiant and over-compliant. In the more passive manifestation of preoccupied attachment, a child will deploy a uniform helplessness, which hides her aggression completely. This exaggerated fearfulness is also known as compulsive care-seeking; we see the harm it does in clients whose lives are defined in terms of problems requiring assistance.

Clearly, the "choice" of strategy is made in response to existing family dynamics because the child is adaptive and will evolve the strategy that gets best results—that is, maximum access and proximity to the caregiver. Almost always, there will be some oscillation between the two poles and when this oscillation is very severe, we would describe the individual as borderline.

Culture

I want to think briefly about patients who defy classification. Some people have particularly mixed patterns—perhaps being strongly dismissing with one parent and preoccupied with the other. Another group I believe do have a predominant style but it has been overlaid and disguised so that they, in effect, have a deceptive attachment pattern which can divert us from understanding them. Culture and class impact strongly on the ways in which attachment patterns manifest, and a notable instance of this happens when a child with an anxious ambivalent pattern is raised in a very strict environment. This authoritarian setting might be the child's actual home or it might be a boarding school. In either case, the child learns to be very polite and these "good" manners, especially in boys and men, can go a long way to disguising the preoccupied style. "Boarding school syndrome" has been powerfully described by Schaverien (2015), but the domestic version of this is not quite so well documented. I have in mind clients from families where the parenting values were authoritarian (Baumrind, 1971) while the attachment was inconsistent and collusive. These clients have an additional inner torment, being torn between the dictates of attachment needs and those of a behavioural code. A child with a more dismissing strategy may cope rather better with the behavioural code because it is aligned with their own internal defensive structures. For the child with a preoccupied strategy, internal and external are in conflict: their fear of abandonment prompts them to signal distress and to "cry for help", while their need to conform forbids this. In raising the theme of boarding school, it would be wrong to convey the impression that avoidant, dismissing behaviour is the preserve of the economically privileged. Van IJzendoorn and Bakermans-Kranenburg found that:

> low SES [socio-economic status] adolescent mothers showed the strongest over-representation of dismissing attachments, which supports the life history theory prediction that in harsh environments individuals adopt a quantity-oriented reproductive strategy in tandem with a dismissing view of attachment.
>
> (2010, p. 200)

Although researchers assure us that attachment patterns are distributed equally across gender lines (Van IJzendoorn & Bakermans-Kranenburg, 2010), it is often remarked that preoccupied traits have some correspondence with our traditional gender stereotype of a woman. We may wonder how this colours the specific experience of being a man or a woman with preoccupied style in our society. Perhaps a man with this pattern may feel he only "passes" as a man and that part of him is effeminate. A risk for a woman is that she feels she matches the misogynistic view of women as hysterical and dependent. How would this work in couples? If we meet a heterosexual couple where the woman seems quite nervous and distressed about the relationship and the man appears calmer and speaks in a pedantic way, then our first impression might peg her as the pursuer and him as the pursued. If we then learn more about how they fight, we might discover that he is persistent in demanding her attention, while she just longs to get away from his "picking". Or we could imagine another heterosexual couple where her manner is cool and inscrutable whilst his is friendly and smiley. From the description so far, we know nothing about their respective attachment patterns but we might expect that she is more dismissing and he is the more preoccupied. In fact, the reverse could be true: that she is anxious about abandonment and he is more anxious about intrusion, she escalates feelings and he minimises them. In therapy, she will need more help with containment and he with the thawing out of a high-functioning false self.

Countertransference and empathy

I will look first at the elements that can make countertransference particularly challenging in work with this group, and then at strategies that can help us sustain empathy alongside the uncomfortable negative feelings that may be evoked by a client's demanding or dependent behaviour.

With all the clients whom we see, there will be some parts of the self that are more visible and others that are more deeply buried; however, for people with preoccupied strategies, the connection between the "presented self" and the authentic self can be particularly hard to keep in mind. The central bind, which can entrap both the preoccupied person and their significant other, is that they are chronically signalling distress in a way that will get some response but that does not accurately represent their pain. Unless we can decode this, then the authentic distress beneath will remain hidden.

Anecdote of Mike and James, who were seen as a couple

Mike is quite preoccupied and a "pursuer" and his partner James is the "withdrawer". Mike complained of having to tiptoe around James; he sighed in a theatrical way as he justified his restrained way of coping with James's "difficult" behaviour. I asked about this tiptoe experience, saying something like, "How does James know you are tiptoeing?", and Mike immediately felt accused and snapped at me. With hindsight, I see that there *was* something accusatory in me, as though I were imagining that what Mike called "tiptoeing" could in fact be aggravating to James. Fortunately, I realised that I had gone in the wrong direction, I had responded to Mike's angry, blaming complaint by retreating from Mike myself. My enquiry was inviting him to step back into an abstracted kind of reflection; he resented that I was not attending to his experience. I changed direction and moved in to validate his feelings, recognising how hard he had to work with James, how thankless that could feel, and how endless the task could seem. The change in Mike was obvious, he sighed deeply, his body relaxed, and then he spoke in a soft, reflective voice. Now all three of us were directly connecting to the deep sadness about the relationship and the longing for connection that was so often broken. Mike himself could recognise and feel the difference between the deep sigh he had just made and the angry righteous sighs a minute earlier.

Listening to that vignette of Mike and James and seeing how much better things go when authentic emotions are shared, we might ask why a person with preoccupied strategy keeps on resorting to the display feelings that actually yield such a poor outcome? In addition to the basic tendency to go on doing what we have always done, there are three particularly strong factors that maintain the pattern and that we aim to address in therapy:

1. The impulse to signal distress is like a familiar reflex—whereas the internal pathway to reach the primary feelings is much harder to find. In the room, we will often be using the "pause" button to help the client slow down at that moment when they are drawn to the comfortable option of presenting their display feelings—whether that is the coercive aggression or the coercive helplessness described by Crittenden and colleagues (2014).
2. The primary emotions feel too scary because the person never had help with these as a child. If we and the client can collaborate to work the pause button, then we will have a chance to sit with the authentic emotions, which may then come into view. Learning that these can be tolerated will build resilience and options.
3. These display feelings became so established as a pattern because they got the best results in early years. We will be aiming to provide clients with a novel response. While a coercive helplessness may sometimes prompt in us the same rescuing reflex that it once evoked in parents and teachers, we aim to bring a more thoughtful response along with that, so that clients are met with a disconfirming response (Bernier & Dozier, 2002; Bowlby, 1988).

Primary and secondary feelings

To try to make sense of this dichotomy between primary and secondary affects, I'm going to reach beyond attachment theory. Transactional analysis has conceptualised this split in terms of authentic feelings and rackety feelings. Stewart describes how a racket feeling is a stand-in: "A racket feeling always acts as a substitute for another feeling that was prohibited in the family of origin" (1989, p. 67). Transactional analysis offers quite specific criteria for distinguishing between the two sets of emotions, so we may notice the following when racket feelings are operating:

1. Our countertransference—in response to racket feelings, the therapist is likely to feel either irritated or too easily gratified.
2. The repetitive nature of the dynamic.
3. There is often a one-up or one-down quality between the therapist and the client.
4. Racket feelings happen outside their time zone.

In contrast, authentic emotions are informative and may prompt us to solve a problem. Authentic sadness is about the past—I need to mourn; authentic anger is about the present—I need to assert myself; authentic fear is about the future—I need to take preventative action (Stewart, 1989).

If we apply these criteria, we can see that the activity of "complaining" can be used as an effective defence against real pain. As chronic complaining can also have a deadening effect on the therapist, it may serve to distract her from tuning into the authentic pain, at the same time that it distracts and occupies the client.

The subject of complaining is explored by Weintrobe, although in the terms she uses, my last paragraph would be referring to a *grievance* rather than a *complaint*. I think her two categories illustrate what I am calling the authentic and the displayed emotions. She suggests that complaint is based on "lively entitlement", which she contrasts strongly with the narcissistic entitlement of grievance. Weintrobe suggests that while "The grievance can be clung to and nursed like a babe in arms" (2004, p. 84), a complaint is made by someone who knows their own separateness. This understanding about lack of separation and the exaggerated nursing of a grievance points to two key elements in preoccupied experience: enmeshment with a parent, and escalation or amplification of feelings. Weintrobe also points us to the links with Freud's "Mourning and melancholia" (1917), which serves as an early description of preoccupied grieving. She writes:

> Nursing the grievance keeps alive the possibility of restoring the relationship with the idealised object, if not now, then at some point in the future.
>
> (2004, p. 84)

Her advice for how to speak to the client about this is very precise: we must speak to both levels.

> If interpreting narcissistic features can happen alongside and in the same context of interpreting liveliness, it may feel more bearable to the analysand.
>
> (2004, p. 91)

When we respond to people with preoccupied strategies, it helps if we can name both levels at once—the deeper, aching pain that is really not expressed, as well as the manipulative, performed affect that is often over-expressed.

Therapeutic empathy

Given the challenging dynamic that arises with a preoccupied client, how do we sustain an empathic connection? On the one hand, we need to feel the frustration and irritation at how we are being positioned and used as an audience; at the same time, we want to remain compassionate. In my learning curve with these patients, my struggle has been to sustain empathy. In my opening anecdote, I described how my irritated countertransference overwhelmed me, and when the client said he was leaving I was glad to give up the effort of sustaining it. I think what has changed for me since then is my deeper understanding of the bind that people with preoccupied strategies have to manage.

Like a traveller who never finds their destination, or a hungry person who does find food but is unable to swallow, they have the experience of being destined to seek help from which they can never benefit. I searched for images or stories that could convey this and found nothing that is as powerful for me as the iconic attachment moment where the child who has demanded to be picked up immediately arches their body away from their parent. I think the myth of Sisyphus relentlessly pushing his boulder conveys some of the misery, as does the task of repainting the Forth rail bridge (before the recent application of a special epoxy coating, this re-painting task was said to be ceaseless).

The child who cannot relax into the safety of a parental hug is not getting that lovely ventral/ventral contact by which the human being, young or old, draws maximum comfort from touch. In contrast to the arching away of the preoccupied child, we see the snug contact that the secure infant achieves in moulding to the parent's body, relaxing into maximum contact with that other body, providing wordless regulation—one parasympathetic system to another.

Crittenden and colleagues express the cruel paradox:

> Ironically the children who seem most effective at getting parental attention often seem least satisfied with what they get. Maybe this is because they know that their parents' attention must be maintained and that their real need, that of knowing that their parents are in control and able to evaluate and meet their children's needs, is unfulfilled.
>
> (Crittenden, Dallos, Landini, & Kozlowska, 2014, p. 77)

The child with this strategy cannot take in the soothing for which she longs because all her energy is focused on making the demand. If she lets up on the protest and crying, she fears her mother's attention will again be lost.

What do we do in the room to help preoccupied clients?

Earlier, I identified three key strategies for working with preoccupied clients:

- Using the pause button when racket feelings are escalating.
- Demonstrating that authentic feelings can be tolerated by sitting with them and validating them.
- Disconfirming the client's expectation of either rescue or abandonment.

Clients with preoccupied strategies, whether blaming or demanding, are used to meeting with quite negative responses, and clearly it is important that we break the mould of this expectation. The structure of the sessions helps us contain these demands, and we hope then to be able to access the primary feelings that lie behind the presented anger or helplessness. This is well described by attachment writers:

> The therapist validates secondary reactive affect and helps differentiate and expand this affect until primary attachment emotions and associated appraisals emerge and can be coherently stated.
>
> (Johnson & Whiffen, 1999, p. 375)

> we need to respond to the deeper feelings that underlie the patient's displays of distress.
>
> (Wallin, 2007, p. 226)

Because the display feelings are so engaging, we will sometimes enter an enactment—we might obey the "stage direction" given to us by the patient's projective identification. Because the client is expecting the "Other" to be abandoning and blaming, and herself to be a victim, the therapist may act this out, if only by making a distancing, top-down interpretation, which is a form of detachment and accusation. We saw this earlier in my first anecdote (I gave away the patient's time slot) and in the second (I initially responded to Mike with a withdrawal).

Writers who help us discern how to work with clients of different attachment styles

Contemporary writers support Bowlby's (1988) thesis that clients with insecure attachment are most helped by a disconfirming response from their therapists. Johnson and Whiffen write:

> change in relationships is assumed to arise from compelling emotional experiences that disconfirm past fears and biases and allow working models to be elaborated and revised.
>
> (1999, p. 372)

We know that when our own insecurity is evoked by a very disturbed client, we are more at risk of making a confirming response. In such a case, unfortunately, we might move in closer to a client with a preoccupied pattern, offering the "reassurance" their rackety feelings demand; in response to the cool presentation of someone with a dismissing style, we might increase distance through discursive or cognitive interventions.

Bernier and Dozier have looked at counsellor/client pairs and have established that when therapist and client have dissimilar or contrasting personal relational styles, this has a better outcome:

> the therapist's natural stance helps him or her resist the pull to adopt a reinforcing position in response to the client's rigid and maladaptive relational patterns.
>
> (2002, p. 33)

Although it is ultimately helpful, in the short run this non-complementary behaviour does raise anxiety. Getting the "right amount" of anxiety and containment is the holy grail of therapy. In Vygotsky's terms, we are aiming for the zone of proximal development where there is enough safety to enable exploration and enough challenge to permit growth. Heard and Lake (1997) suggest that the aim of the attachment therapist is to move responsively between more supportive and more exploratory/interpretive forms of relating. This balancing act is described poetically by a number of theorists. Hardy and Aldridge put it well: "where the unknown is experienced but contained" (1999, p. 37). Similarly poetic, Josephs asks "How do we avoid the twin dangers of either being a 'bull in a china shop' or of handling the patient with 'kid gloves'?" (1997, p. 5).

Daly and Mallinckrodt (2009) offer a model for therapeutic distance that indicates how a therapist enables a dismissing patient to move towards intimacy and a preoccupied one to achieve more autonomy. They illustrate this with a diagram showing the relative positions of the two parties over the life of the therapy. The result for the preoccupied patient and her therapist is the outline of a Christmas tree: initially, at the apex of the tree, the therapist matches the patient's need for closeness, but over time they are able to increase therapeutic distance, arriving at the wider base. For the dismissing patient, the diagram looks like a vase with a wide mouth and a narrow base: the dyad start off far apart but move nearer together as tolerance of closeness increases.

Countertransference pitfalls

I have indicated several points at which I have struggled with my feelings in relation to people with preoccupied strategies, but of course I must acknowledge that these moments I have digested and shared with you are the conscious part of my story. By definition, I cannot accurately convey what has passed me by. ... perhaps times when I have been governed by my feelings without realising; or perhaps times when I have flattened out the landscape between the client and myself so that I was not available to be imprinted with her experience. Kantrowitz sums up the two essential capacities:

> Unless the analyst experiences an emotional intensity, the affective reliving will not occur. The analyst must also have the capacity to observe what occurs between them and to tolerate the intense affects that are generated.
>
> (1995, p. 302)

Wallin has a number of helpful comments about the challenges that arise when the therapist's defensive strategies are triggered. He specifically suggests that a therapist with more avoidant traits may be tempted into unhelpful activity:

> Rather than resonate with the patient's deeper feelings—or notice the lack of fit between what is being said and what seems to be felt.... we may choose to help by trying to "corral" the patient's intense emotion with intellectual understanding.
>
> (2007, p. 232)

Slade makes a similar observation about the temptation to step in and get the patient's story sorted out.

> patients who are primarily preoccupied with respect to attachment are trying to get the therapist to lessen their sense of confusion and take care of them, and yet collaboration with the therapist is all but impossible for these patients. And the therapist feels much the way the patient once did as a child: swamped, angry, helpless, confused and dysregulated .... And, in natural response to becoming mired in such feelings, a therapist will often try to organise and structure a preoccupied patient.
>
> (1999, p. 588)

Wallin suggests that therapists with more preoccupied traits may empathise more readily but are more at risk of being pulled into a rescuer role.

While erotic feelings in the transference or countertransference may arise with clients of any attachment orientation and need to be thought about in each relationship, Wallin points out a way that preoccupied clients may mobilise erotic energy in the room.

> Sometimes the erotic transference is an important waystation for the preoccupied patient en route to the development of a deeper capacity to trust and to love. But if the therapist is either too pleased or too discomfited by the patient's desire, that welcome development may be thwarted.
>
> (2007, p. 234)

Wallin's observation chimes with the research indicates that people with preoccupied strategies favour sex as a route to closeness, whereas those with dismissing patterns are more likely to enjoy a more aloof kind of sex that minimises closeness (Feeney, 1999).

Loss and mourning—chronic and complicated grief

Freud's 1917 paper "Mourning and melancholia" tells us a lot about how preoccupied people cope with the tasks of mourning. He describes how the anger and ambivalence that belong to that lost relationship are turned against the self, and the connection to the dead person is held to as an ideal. Perhaps the difference a hundred years on is that at that point Freud was writing as though there could be a "correct" or completed form of mourning in which the bereaved person makes a clean break with the lost loved one. We know Freud himself evolved his ideas on this, and we have come to understand mourning as more nuanced:

> Mourning is a complicated task that requires the living to assimilate the loss, maintain a positive internal connection to the lost person, and continue to find meaning in other areas of life.
>
> (Adelman & Malawista, 2013, p. 9)

Klein's understanding of mourning may also throw light on the experience of people with preoccupied strategies. She sees adult mourning as a revisiting of the time when the young infant has lost the breast-mother:

> Just as the young child passing through the depressive position is struggling, in his unconscious mind, with the task of establishing

and integrating his inner world, so the mourner goes through the
pain of re-establishing and re-integrating it.

>   (Klein, 1940, in Mitchell, 1986, p. 156)

She reminds us that mourning is so alarming because we fear to lose
our internal objects along with the external, and I think her observa-
tions apply particularly to a mourner with preoccupied patterns who
wants to cling to the lost person and who has had to manage an extreme
degree of ambivalence toward the attachment figure. Klein's understanding of the capacity for gratitude can also throw light on the difficulty that preoccupied people have with grief. Here, she describes the
fulfilled and loving experience of a secure infant.

> A full gratification at the breast means that the infant feels he has
> received from his loved object a unique gift, which he wants to
> keep. This is the basis for gratitude. Gratitude includes belief in
> good objects and trust in them. It includes the ability to assimilate
> the loved object—not only as a source of food—and to love it with-
> out envy and interfering.
>
>   (Klein, 1956, in Mitchell, 1986, p. 215)

People with preoccupied strategies can rarely enjoy the feeling
of gratitude; if we are in a preoccupied state with our attachment
relationships, to be grateful would risk signalling that things are
good enough, and this could seem to almost invite abandonment.
Gratitude is about having the capacity *both* to know we are benefiting *and* to enjoy that. The individual with strong preoccupied traits is
condemned always to be scanning for where the next meal is coming
from, never to be sitting calmly and basking in the pleasure of what
is currently to hand.

Other writers who illustrate the experience of loss for a preoccupied person, while not referring explicitly to attachment patterns, are
Adelman and Malawista. They describe:

> extensive periods of rumination … a continual revisiting of the
> death. This type of depression prevents painful emotions from
> transforming or being repaired. Instead, the bereaved remains
> frozen at the threshold of loss, unable to work through the death.
>
>   (2013, p. 6)

And later, they add an additional detail, which belongs with this description of preoccupied grief:

> At times we find we are loath to give up the pain of loss because it binds us still to whom or what we've lost.
>
> (2013, p. 11)

* * *

Stroebe and Schut (2001) have introduced us to the idea of mourning as an oscillation between loss and restoration, and they argue that it is the capacity to move between the two states that helps us mourn and move on. We need the sad times when we are immersed in the pain, but we also need space for positive re-appraisal and moving on. This rhythm is important because it helps us recognise the loss, while protecting us from overwhelming despair. Their research matches Adelman and Malawista's poetic description of the ebb and flow of pain:

> The mourner can begin to integrate the reality and finality of the loss in small doses that ebb and flow in and out of our awareness.
>
> (2013, p. 11)

Stroebe and Schut found that people with a more ruminative style in early bereavement were more likely to be depressed six months on, while those with more a distractive style were less depressed (2001, p. 4). They hypothesise more precisely as to how ruminative thinking may prolong grief, suggesting that it exaggerates the effect of negative mood, intrudes into active, instrumental behaviour, and interferes with effective problem-solving.

Ending therapy

If therapy has been deeply healing and has lasted many years, the ending forces us into a strange corner: in which other circumstances would we voluntarily break off, with finality, a relationship we have valued highly and which has touched us so deeply? For a patient who has lived with a preoccupied attachment strategy and who still manages residual ambivalent traits, this will be particularly testing. If the ending is not voluntary but has been imposed because the therapist is ill, retiring, relocating, or closing her practice for any other reason, then clients are likely to experience a rejection, and there will be much to process. Murdin puts it starkly: "The illusion of unity and control is shattered" (2000, p. 82), pointing us to Winnicott's understanding about the need for gradual disillusionment as the mother presents reality to the growing infant at a pace that is bearable (1969).

In my research into therapists who were closing a practice and thus imposing an ending on their clients (Power, 2016), I heard interesting cases of patients with different attachment strategies, but perhaps most striking were those therapists who spoke about how their own attachment stories impacted on their process. Holmes (1997) has made a useful point about regular endings: that therapists with residual avoidant traits may tend to cut off too soon with their clients, while more ambivalent therapists might hold on too long. My interviewees indicated how this might look when it comes to the therapist's last goodbye and an ending is being imposed on all remaining clients. One of my interviewees, Patsy, was able to voice how retirement may bring us face to face with our deeper reasons for entering the profession, and how the retired therapist is losing her chosen way of managing those discomforts within the self. She reflected that amongst her motivations for being a therapist, her wish to heal her depressed mother was pre-eminent. To give up on that calling was very hard.

Somehow it has felt like [I'm] abandoning my mother.

If we have chosen this work to meet our need to be useful, then it will be very hard for us ever to feel that we have done enough.

It's easier to retire when you feel you've done a good job. Perhaps staying on and on and never retiring is because therapists are after that elusive feeling of doing good, rather than have to face what they haven't done.

Ending imposed by the therapist moving away

A younger therapist, Zoe, was in her forties and was closing a small private practice to move to another part of the country. Zoe, a supervisee, kindly gave me permission to use her story—the client has been fictionalised. The move was prompted by her partner's change of job, and Zoe was able to give her clients nine months' notice; she had some mixed feelings about the move, being broadly happy about it but also a bit resentful for being forced into a decision. She had briefly wondered whether she might return to her home town one day a week to see clients.

The client Sarah was also in her forties and had been seeing Zoe weekly for over three years. She had come to counselling because she feared she might be suffering from PTSD. Her painful memories of childhood and her accounts of relationships, both personal and professional, indicated a strong preoccupied pattern; disappointment was a predominant feeling and this was also expressed towards Zoe.

News of departure

When Zoe explained that she would be moving away and they would have to end the work, Sarah's initial response was to say that she had been thinking of finishing anyway, much sooner than that, as she thought she'd done what she needed. Zoe felt that, by aiming this kick at her, Sarah was protecting herself against the potential pain of being left; over subsequent weeks, she tried to encourage Sarah to keep exploring how the imposed ending might be impacting. We wondered about Sarah's reluctance to reflect on Zoe's leaving her, and we understood this as her defence against a cascade of bad feelings associated with being left: feelings of low self-esteem, impotence, and rage as her fear of rejection came true again. We also understood that Zoe's own slightly mixed feelings about the move didn't incline her to the task of helping clients to connect to their anger and sadness. Perhaps in desperation, I encouraged anything that could sneak past Sarah's defences and stir up her curiosity about the ending—including systemic questions: "If you were having a conversation, in six weeks' or six months' time, about the counselling, what might you be saying about it?" Sarah's sessions proceeded, she did not leave, she continued to come very regularly, and her disappointment with her life and the people around her remained a feature in what she brought to the counselling. She often considered walking out of relationships and situations that she found difficult but always stopped short of actually doing so. In supervision, we thought a lot about how effective Sarah's denial of the ending was; we both felt there must be distress about losing Zoe, and this was very obliquely represented in her complaints about other significant relationships.

At the penultimate session, things changed dramatically

Sarah was tearful and angry as she said she had hoped to be better by the time of ending, and instead she was feeling very panicked about her job and was waking anxious each day. Zoe was dismayed to be finally faced with Sarah's distress at the eleventh hour and, perhaps in her own panic, seized on a way out and reminded Sarah that they had spoken of the possibility of her joining a support group. Sarah became more angry, taking this as an accusation that she could not cope. She was resentful of the idea that she might benefit from further professional help when her time with Zoe should have made her better. She accused Zoe of being no help at all—that more than that, it had been a complete waste of her time and money.

When the session ended, Zoe realised that she was now feeling profoundly burdened and guilty for having failed Sarah. She felt extremely anxious about how to handle the final session, and the next day she woke with a knot in her stomach—a kind of sick fear. She thought of contacting me, feeling the need to talk over the final session and the desperate wish to produce what would satisfy Sarah. She was able to think of her anxiety as countertransference (I think more specifically, we could say projective identification because the client's feelings had been transferred, like a spell, into the therapist). Zoe was also able to have the positive thought that if she could handle this alone she might be modelling something for Sarah [despite her process not being consciously known by Sarah] and that this might in some way support Sarah's capacity to cope alone, which she would now have to do after the final session. She sensed that in accusing her of being a rubbish counsellor, Sarah was conveying the horrible disappointment she felt towards herself, in so many areas.

In the final session, Zoe's thinking paid off

Sarah arrived at the session in tears, and she cried on and off through the hour. The grip of the preoccupied defence had been loosened, and she was able to let Zoe see her appreciation, as well as her sadness and even an increased sense of autonomy. Sarah was able to accept that further counselling could be useful one day, but actually expressed some hope and excitement about managing by herself. She could openly voice what could have been better. This did not seem to be a reproach but a sadness about her part in not making as much use of the space as she would have liked to. Finally, in what seemed like a coded message of gratitude to Zoe, Sarah

disclosed that an old family friend had recently helped her in a very significant way. This good news had been positively withheld from Zoe, but on
the last day it seemed as though Sarah could risk this position of gratitude
towards her family and indicate that Zoe had been useful.

What is this story telling us about the client/counsellor fit?

The absorption by Zoe of the panicked and desperate feelings was a
dramatic moment and it seemed very useful to Sarah that Zoe was
able to manage these by herself. This is the therapeutic process working effectively: the therapist is hit hard by the client's feelings, she is
temporarily overwhelmed, but soon able to bring her thinking to bear
on the countertransference. How might our own attachment, and our
attachment fit with the client, impact on both these stages? What makes
us accessible to those parts which the client wants to export? Would
a counsellor with a more dismissing pattern have been less accessible
than Zoe?

It is hard for us to know when an ending is "good enough", but
this one gave reason to hope. What might have happened afterwards?
We hope that those challenging parts of Sarah did not suddenly
return and knock her for six. Perhaps in an ideal world, we would find
a way in to name what was happening and to link up the two different
states that seemed so separate. "It's as though an angry and perhaps
young part of you was very present last week—you needed to let me
know how bad it felt to be disappointed. And as though this week a
stronger part of you can enjoy letting me know that I have helped you."
Or, "We both know that the hurting angry part has not completely
packed her bags; we know that today you are calmer and can allow
that something good came from your family friend. We have learnt
that your distress can be understood without that blaming part of you
taking charge."

Conclusion

We have spent a day reflecting on work with people who manage themselves and others with preoccupied strategies, and I think this has indicated how helpful it can be to recognise a client's predominant way of
relating, but I think we would say it is not necessary. There will be cases
where we cannot discern a predominant pattern, and perhaps the value

of the question then is not the answer but the process of enquiry, which may sharpen our curiosity and deepen our commitment to understanding and reaching this person.

Whether or not we believe we have identified a client's attachment strategy, we work with an awareness of their need for a secure base, looking for that optimum balance between empathy and exploration—containing the pain but also pushing the client beyond the strategies to which they have clung.

In a way, all therapy is about mourning and, as Holmes has argued, about helping clients get their stories into a more viable shape. Writing about endings, he says:

> The task is not so much to get it right, as to use the ending as a powerful exemplar from which the client can learn about the ways his or her unconscious shapes the way he or she handles and has handled, loss and separation.
>
> (2010, p. 70)

Klein reminds us of the link between mourning and gratitude, and of the strong correspondence between secure attachment and the capacity for gratitude.

> every advance in the process of mourning results in a deepening in the individual's relation to his inner objects, in the happiness of regaining them after they were felt to be lost … in an increased trust in them and love for them.
>
> (Klein, 1940, in Mitchell, 1986, p. 164)

* * *

When the work goes well and a client's preoccupied strategy can be relaxed, hypervigilance will reduce, and they will begin to take the risk of staying with good feelings. Authentic feelings can be trusted; display feelings will feel less necessary. Instead of an arching away, there is a leaning in, and there is more of a self that can be trusted and loved. This might not be quite Klein's happiness of regaining what was felt to be lost—because that phrase suggests return to a golden age. This journey is about going to parts of the self that formerly we felt we had to avoid, and finding that they can be loved.

References

Adelman, A. J., & Malawista, K. L. (2013). *The Therapist in Mourning: From the Faraway Nearby*. New York: Columbia University Press.

Baumrind, D. (1971). Current patterns of parental authority. *Developmental Psychology, 4*: 1–103.

Bernier, A., & Dozier, M. (2002). The client-counselor match and the corrective emotional experience: evidence from interpersonal and attachment research. *Psychotherapy: Theory, Research, Training, 39*(1): 32–43.

Bowlby, J. (1973). *Attachment and Loss*, Volume 2: *Separation, Anger and Anxiety*. London: Hogarth Press & Institute of Psycho-Analysis.

Bowlby, J. (1988). *A Secure Base: Clinical Applications of Attachment Theory*. London: Tavistock/Routledge.

Crittenden, P., Dallos, R., Landini, A., & Kozlowska, K. (2014). *Attachment and Family Therapy*. Maidenhead: Open University Press.

Daly, K. D., & Mallinckrodt, B. (2009). Experienced therapists' approach to psychotherapy for adults with attachment avoidance or attachment anxiety. *Journal of Counseling Psychology, 56*(4): 549–563.

Feeney, J. A. (1999). Adult romantic attachment and couple relationships. In: J. Cassidy & P. R. Shaver (Eds.), *Handbook of Attachment: Theory, Research, and Clinical Applications* (pp. 355–377). New York: Guilford Press.

Freud, S. (1917e). Mourning and melancholia. *S. E., 14*: 237–258. London: Hogarth.

Hardy, G. E., & Aldridge, J. (1999). Therapist responsiveness to client attachment styles and issues observed in client-identified significant events in psychodynamic-interpersonal psychotherapy. *Psychotherapy Research, 9*(1): 36–53.

Heard, D., & Lake, B. (1997). *The Challenge of Attachment for Caregiving*. London: Routledge.

Holmes, J. (1997). "Too early, too late": endings in psychotherapy—an attachment perspective. *British Journal of Psychotherapy, 14*(2): 159–174.

Holmes, J. (2010). Termination in psychoanalytic psychotherapy: an attachment perspective. In: J. Salberg (Ed.), *Good Enough Endings: Breaks, Interruptions and Terminations from Contemporary Relational Perspectives* (pp. 63–82). New York: Routledge.

Johnson, S. M., & Whiffen, V. E. (1999). Made to measure: adapting emotionally focused couple therapy to partners' attachment styles. *Clinical Psychology: Science and Practice, 6*(4): 366–381.

Josephs, L. (1997). Balancing empathy and interpretation in the analytic process. *Issues in Psychoanalytic Psychology, 19*: 5–26.

Kantrowitz, J. L. (1995). The beneficial aspects of the patient–analyst match. *The International Journal of Psycho-Analysis, 76*(2): 299.

Klein, M. (1940). Mourning and manic-depressive states. In: J. Mitchell (Ed.), *The Selected Melanie Klein*. New York: The Free Press, 1986.

Klein, M. (1956). A study of envy and gratitude. In: J. Mitchell (Ed.), *The Selected Melanie Klein*. New York: The Free Press, 1986.

Mikulincer, M., & Shaver, P. R. (2010). Does gratitude promote prosocial behaviour? The moderating role of attachment security. In: M. Mikulincer & P. R. Shaver (Eds.), *Prosocial Motives, Emotions and Behavior: The Better Angels of Our Nature* (pp. 267–283). Washington, DC: American Psychological Association.

Murdin, L. (2000). *How Much Is Enough? Endings in Psychotherapy and Counselling*. London: Routledge.

Power, A. (2015). *Forced Endings in Psychotherapy and Psychoanalysis: Attachment and Loss in Retirement*. Hove: Routledge.

Schaverien, J. (2015). *Boarding School Syndrome: The Psychological Trauma of the "Privileged" Child*. Hove: Routledge.

Slade, A. (1999). Attachment theory and research: implications for the theory and practice of individual psychotherapy with adults. In: J. Cassidy & P. R. Shaver (Eds.), *Handbook of Attachment: Theory, Research and Clinical Applications* (pp. 575–594). New York: Guilford Press.

Stewart, I. (1986). *Transactional Analysis in Action*. London: Sage.

Stroebe, M. S., & Schut, H. (2001). Meaning-making in the dual process model of coping with bereavement. In: R. A. Neimeyer (Ed.), *Meaning Reconstruction and the Experience of Loss* (pp. 55–73). Washington, DC: American Psychological Association.

Van IJzendoorn, M. H., & Bakermans-Kranenburg, M. J. (2010). Invariance of adult attachment across gender, age, culture, and socioeconomic status? *Journal of Social and Personal Relationships, 27*(2): 200–208.

Vygotsky, L. (1978). Interaction between learning and development. *Readings on the Development of Children, 23*(3): 34–41.

Wallin, D. J. (2007). *Attachment in Psychotherapy*. New York: Guilford Press.

Weintrobe, S. (2004). Links between grievance, complaint and different forms of entitlement. *International Journal of Psychoanalysis, 85*: 83–96.

Winnicott, D. W. (1969). The use of an object. *The International Journal of Psycho-Analysis, 50*: 711.

INDEX

For Product Safety Concerns and Information please contact our EU
representative GPSR@taylorandfrancis.com
Taylor & Francis Verlag GmbH, Kaufingerstraße 24, 80331 München, Germany

www.ingramcontent.com/pod-product-compliance
Lightning Source LLC
Chambersburg PA
CBHW050537270326
41926CB00015B/3271